Worlds of Wonder

We use imagination to explore and explain the world.

SCHOLASTIC

LITERACY PLACE®

Copyright acknowledgments and credits appear on page 136, which constitutes an extension of this copyright page.

Copyright © 1996 by Scholastic Inc.   All rights reserved.   Printed in the U.S.A.
                                             ISBN 0-590-49117-2
          2 3 4 5 6 7 8 9 10   24   02 01 00 99 98 97 96

Explore

a Movie Studio

We use imagination to explore and explain the world.

Timeless Tales

Throughout history, people have used stories to entertain and explain.

Fantastic Voyages

Stories present faraway worlds and remarkable characters.

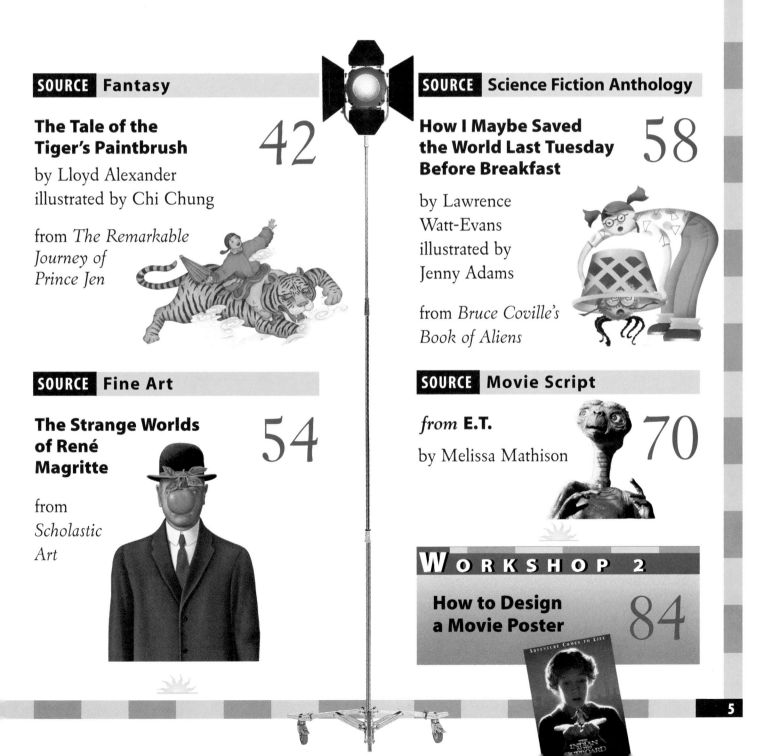

Coming Attractions

**Creative talent brings
fantastic stories to life.**

Trade Books

The following books accompany this *Worlds of Wonder* SourceBook.

Myths

AWARD WINNING Book

Favorite Greek Myths

by Mary Pope Osborne
illustrated by Troy Howell

FAVORITE GREEK MYTHS

RETOLD BY MARY POPE OSBORNE
ILLUSTRATED BY TROY HOWELL

Science Fiction

AWARD WINNING Author

The Lost Star

by H.M. Hoover

The Lost Star
H. M. Hoover

SCHOLASTIC

Fantasy

AWARD WINNING Book

The Phantom Tollbooth

by Norton Juster
illustrated by Jules Feiffer

THE PHANTOM TOLLBOOTH

NORTON JUSTER
Illustrations by JULES FEIFFER

Fiction

AWARD WINNING Book

Tuck Everlasting

by Natalie Babbitt

Tuck Everlasting
NATALIE BABBITT

SCHOLASTIC

Throughout history, people have used stories to entertain and explain.

Timeless Tales

Explore the world of Greek mythology, when you read two tales that have lasted through the ages. Next read a poem about Native American traditions.

Discover where the expression "sour grapes" comes from, and why ants always work hard. Then learn about Anansi, the clever trickster.

WORKSHOP 1

Write a fable that illustrates an important lesson.

THE CAMEL DANCES

The Camel had her heart set on becoming a ballet dancer.
"To make every movement a thing of grace and beauty,"
said the Camel, "That is my one and only desire."
Again and again she practiced her pirouettes, her relevés,
and her arabesques. She repeated the five basic positions a
hundred times each day. She worked for long months under
the hot desert sun. Her feet were blistered, and her body
ached with fatigue, but not once did she think of stopping.
At last the Camel said, "Now I am a dancer," she announced
a recital, and danced before an invited group of camel friends
and critics. When her dance was over, she made a deep bow.
There was no applause.
"I must tell you frankly," said a member of the audience,
"as a critic and a spokesman for this group, that you are
lumpy and bumpy. You are baggy and bumpy. You are, like
the rest of us, simply a camel. You are not and never will be
a ballet dancer!"
Chuckling and laughing, the audience moved away across
the sand.
"How very wrong they are!" said the Camel. "I have worked
hard. There can be no doubt that I am a splendid dancer. I will
dance and dance just for myself."
That is what she did. It gave her many years of pleasure.

Satisfaction will come to those who please themselves.

FAVORITE
GREEK
MYTHS

RETOLD BY
MARY POPE OSBORNE
ILLUSTRATED BY
TROY HOWELL

FROM

FAVORITE GREEK MYTHS

RETOLD BY MARY POPE OSBORNE

ILLUSTRATED BY TROY HOWELL

The stories the ancient Greeks created about
their gods and goddesses are called myths.
Not only did the myths help explain the mysteries
of nature, but they also provided wonderful
entertainment on cold winter nights. As the myths
were passed from generation to generation,
different Greek and Roman
poets retold them.

THE GOLDEN APPLES

The Story of Atalanta and Hippomenes

LONG AGO a baby girl
named Atalanta was left on a wild mountainside because
her father had wanted a boy instead of a girl. A kind bear
discovered the tiny girl and nursed her and cared for her.

And as Atalanta grew up, she lived as the bears lived: eating wild honey and berries and hunting in the woods. Finally as a young woman on her own, she became a follower of Diana, the goddess of wild things. Preferring to live on her own, Atalanta blissfully roamed the shadowy woods and sunlit fields.

The god Apollo agreed with Atalanta's choice to be alone. "You must never marry," he told her one day. "If you do, you will surely lose your own identity."

In spite of her decision never to marry, Atalanta was pursued by many suitors. As men watched her run through the fields and forest, they were struck by her beauty and grace.

Angry at the men for bothering her, Atalanta figured out how to keep them away. "I'll race anyone who wants to marry me!" she announced to the daily throng that pursued her. "Whoever is so swift that he can outrun me will receive the prize of my hand in marriage! But whomever I beat—will die."

Atalanta was certain these harsh conditions would discourage everyone from wanting to marry her. But she was wrong. Her strength and grace were so compelling that many men volunteered to race against her—and all of them lost their lives.

One day, a young stranger, wandering through the countryside, stopped to join a crowd that was watching a race between Atalanta and one of her suitors. When Hippomenes realized the terms of the contest, he was appalled. "No person could be worth such a risk!" he exclaimed. "Only an idiot would try to win her for his wife!"

But when Atalanta sped by, and Hippomenes saw her wild hair flying back from her ivory shoulders and her strong body moving as gracefully as a gazelle, even he was overwhelmed with the desire to be her husband.

"Forgive me," he said to the panting loser being taken away to his death. "I did not know what a prize she was."

When Atalanta was crowned with the wreath of victory, Hippomenes stepped forward boldly and spoke to her before the crowd. "Why do you race against men so slow?" he asked. "Why not race against me? If I defeat you, you will not be disgraced, for I am the great-grandson of Neptune, god of the seas!"

"And if I beat you?" Atalanta asked.

"If you beat me...you will certainly have something to boast about!"

As Atalanta stared at the proud young man, she wondered why the gods would wish one as young and bold as Hippomenes to die. And for the first time, she felt she might rather lose than win. Inexperienced in matters of the heart, she did not realize she was falling in love. "Go, stranger," she said softly. "I'm not worth the loss of your life."

But the crowd, sensing a tremendous race might be about to take place, cheered wildly, urging the two to compete. And since Hippomenes eagerly sought the same, Atalanta was forced to give in. With a heavy heart, she consented to race the young man the next day.

In the pink twilight, alone in the hills, Hippomenes prayed to Venus, the goddess of love and beauty. He asked for help in his race against Atalanta. When Venus heard Hippomenes's prayer, she was only too glad to help him, for she wished to punish the young huntress for despising love.

As if in a dream, Venus led Hippomenes to a mighty tree in the middle of an open field. The tree shimmered with golden leaves and golden apples. Venus told Hippomenes to pluck three of the apples from the tree, and then she told him how to use the apples in his race against Atalanta.

The crowd roared as Atalanta and Hippomenes crouched at the starting line. Under his tunic, Hippomenes hid his three golden apples. When the trumpets sounded, the two shot forward and ran so fast that their bare feet barely touched the sand. They looked as if they could run over the surface of the sea without getting their feet wet—or skim over fields of corn without even bending the stalks.

The crowd cheered for Hippomenes, but Atalanta rushed ahead of him and stayed in the lead. When Hippomenes began to pant, and his chest felt as if it might burst open, he pulled one of the golden apples out from under his tunic and tossed it toward Atalanta.

The gleaming apple hit the sand and rolled across Atalanta's path. She left her course and chased after the glittering ball, and Hippomenes gained the lead.

The crowd screamed with joy; but after Atalanta picked up the golden apple, she quickly made up for her delay and scooted ahead of Hippomenes.

Hippomenes tossed another golden apple. Again, Atalanta left her course, picked up the apple, then overtook Hippomenes.

As Hippomenes pulled out his third apple, he realized this was his last chance. He reared back his arm and hurled the apple as far as he could into a field.

Atalanta watched the golden ball fly through the air; and she hesitated, wondering whether or not she should run after it. Just as she decided not to, Venus touched her heart, prompting her to abandon her course and rush after the glittering apple.

Atalanta took off into the field after the golden apple—and Hippomenes sped toward the finish line.

Hippomenes won Atalanta for his bride, but then he made a terrible mistake: He neglected to offer gifts to Venus to thank her for helping him.

Enraged by his ingratitude, the goddess of love and beauty called upon the moon goddess, Diana, and told her to punish Hippomenes and Atalanta.

As the moon goddess studied the two proud lovers hunting in the woods and fields, she admired their strength and valor, and she decided to turn them into the animals they most resembled.

One night as Atalanta and Hippomenes lay side by side under the moonlight, changes began to happen to their bodies. They grew rough amber coats, and stiff, long claws. And when dawn came, they woke and growled at the early light. Then the thick tails of the two mighty lions swept the ground as they began hunting for their breakfast.

From then on, Atalanta and Hippomenes lived together as lions deep in the woods, and only the moon goddess could tame them. ■

THE WEAVING CONTEST

The Story of Arachne and Minerva

RACHNE, a proud peasant girl, was a wonderful spinner and weaver of wool. The water nymphs journeyed from their rivers and the wood nymphs from their forests just to watch Arachne steep her wool in crimson dyes, then take the long threads in her skillful fingers and weave exquisite tapestries.

"Ah! Minerva must have given you your gift!" declared a wood nymph one day. Minerva was the goddess of weaving and handicrafts.

Arachne threw back her head. "Ha! Minerva has taught me nothing! I've taught myself everything I know!" And with that, she decided to challenge Minerva to a contest. "Let's see which of us should be called 'goddess of the loom'!" she said.

The nymphs covered their mouths, frightened to hear such scorn heaped upon a powerful goddess of Mount Olympus.

Their fears were justified—for Minerva herself was furious when word got back to her about Arachne's conceit. The goddess immediately donned the disguise of an old woman with gray hair and hobbled with a cane to Arachne's cottage.

When Arachne opened her door, Minerva shook her gnarled finger. "If I were you," said the old woman, "I would not compare myself so favorably to the great goddess Minerva. I would feel humble toward her and ask her to pardon my prideful arrogance."

"You silly fool!" said Arachne. "What do you mean by coming to my door and telling me what to do? If that goddess is half so great as the world thinks, let her come here and show me!"

"She is here!" boomed a powerful voice, and before Arachne's eyes, the old woman instantly changed into the goddess Minerva.

Arachne's face flushed with shame. Nevertheless she remained defiant and plunged headlong toward her doom. "Hello, Minerva," she said. "Do you dare to finally weave against me?"

Minerva only glared at the girl, as the nymphs, peeking from behind the trees, cringed to watch such insolence.

"Come in if you like," Arachne said, stepping back from her doorway and bidding the goddess to enter.

Without speaking, Minerva went into the cottage. Servants quickly dashed about, setting up two looms. Then Arachne and Minerva tucked up their long dresses and set to work. Their busy fingers flew back and forth as they each wove rainbows of colors: dark purples, pinks, golds, and crimsons.

Minerva wove a tapestry showing the twelve greatest gods and goddesses of Mount Olympus. But Arachne wove a tapestry showing not only the gods and goddesses, but their adventures also. Then she bordered her magnificent work with flowers and ivy.

The river nymphs and wood nymphs stared in awe at Arachne's tapestry. Her work was clearly better than Minerva's. Even the goddess Envy who haughtily inspected it, said, "There is no flaw."

When she heard Envy's words, Minerva lost her temper. The goddess tore Arachne's tapestry and hit her mercilessly—until disgraced and humiliated, Arachne crawled away and tried to hang herself.

At last, moved to a little pity, Minerva said, "You may live, Arachne, but you will hang forever—and do your weaving in the air!"

Then the vengeful goddess sprinkled Arachne with hellbane; and the girl's hair fell off, and her nose and ears fell off. Her head shrank to a tiny size until she was mostly a giant belly. But her fingers could still weave; and within minutes, Arachne, the first spider on earth, wove the first magnificent web. ■

FROM NAVAJO VISIONS AND VOICES ACROSS THE MESA

STORM

by Shonto Begay

As a young boy, I sat at my mother's loom.
As she wove, we sang many songs and shared many stories.
Some days
I told her of strange new images
I had seen in magazines,
catalogues and product wrappings.
I tried in vain
to talk her into weaving these
new designs. She would smile and tell me she could not.
She would say
her pattern,
the Tonalea Storm Pattern,
was a gift given to her as a young girl.
A gift of a vision from Spider Woman,
a sacred being of mythic times.
She would say her designs were tributes to storm clouds.
They quivered with life and energy.

PATTERN

My mother still weaves fine rugs.
Variations of her storm pattern. Designs flow easily from her fingertips,
designs she coaxes gently
with songs
from deep within.
I laugh now knowing the new images
I tried so hard to interest her in were corporate logos.
I sat for many years at the foot of her loom,
sharing news from magazines and stories from books
she could not read.
Those days of soft thumping of weaving fork and
heddle, voices low, exchanging, sharing, are still with me.
They are woven into my very being.
Corporate logos,
and the bold, sharp-edged storm pattern against a gray sky.

GRANDMOTHER

Grandmother was strong, like a distant mesa.
From her sprang many stories of days long ago.
From her gentle manners
lessons were learned
not easily forgotten.
She told us time and again
that the earth is our mother,
our holy mother.

"Always greet the coming day
by greeting your grandparents,
Yá' át' ééh Shi cheii (Hello, My Grandfather)
to the young juniper tree.
Yá' át' ééh Shi másání (Hello, My Grandmother)
to the young piñon tree."

The lines in her face were marks of honor,
countless winters gazing into the blizzard,
many summers in the hot cornfield.
Her strong brown hands, once smooth,
carried many generations,
gestured many stories,
wiped away many tears.
The whiteness of her windblown hair,
a halo against the setting sun.

My grandmother was called Asdzán Aɫts'íísí,
Small Woman. Wife of Little Hat,
mother of generations of Bitter Water Clan,
she lived 113 years.

from

Aesop's Fables

RETOLD BY

Tom Paxton

ILLUSTRATED BY

Robert Rayevsky

THE FOX AND THE GRAPES

A hungry fox sat under a tree.
(A very high tree,
Yes, a very high tree.)
And up in the tree there grew a vine.
(A very long vine,
Yes, a very long vine.)
And on that vine there grew some grapes.
(They were juicy grapes,
Yes, the juiciest grapes.)
There were grapes on the vine,
On the vine on the tree,
On the tree where the fox
Sat hungrily licking
His ravenous chops,
Saying, "Dinner at last!
I love the shapes,
The color, the taste,
The smell of grapes.
Yes, grapes are a meal that is sure to please,
And the grapes that I crave the most are *these*—
The grapes on the vine,
On the very long vine,
On the vine on the tree.

24

Oh, dinner at last!"
Cried the hungry fox
As he danced a dance,
As he spun a spin,
As he tucked a napkin under his chin.
"Dinner at last!" cried the fox as he
Reached for the grapes in the very high tree,
The grapes that hung so temptingly
Just out of reach in the very high tree.
"Oh blast!" cried the fox as he ran and jumped.
"Oh drat!" cried the fox as he groaned and grumped.
For as high as he sprang, and as much as he strained,
Those juicy grapes were not obtained.
The fox might mutter, shout, and screech,
But still those grapes were out of reach.

At last the hungry fox said, "Now
I'll look elsewhere, and anyhow,"
The fox exclaimed with an icy glower,
"I'm certain that those grapes are sour!"

And, like the fox, we rant and rave
When we can't have the things we crave.
Then, like the fox, we're heard to say
We didn't want them anyway.

THE GRASSHOPPER AND THE ANTS

The grasshopper danced, ta ra, ta ra,
There in the summer sun.
The grasshopper played his violin
And had a world of fun.
The ants, meanwhile, were working hard,
And storing food away;
Puffing and panting day and night,
Laboring night and day.
"Foolish drones!" the grasshopper called,
Turning it into a song.
"Can't you see? There's food enough
To eat the whole day long,
Ta ra," he sang,
"Ta ra," he danced,
"To eat the whole day long."

The grasshopper fiddled his way through June;
He fiddled through July.
He sang and danced all of August away;
September went swiftly by,
Till one cold morning the grasshopper's song
Was heard in the grass no more.
"I don't recall," the grasshopper said,
"Ever being so hungry before.
I say, Mister Ant, it's cold out here,"
The shivering grasshopper said.
He smiled and chirped, "I don't suppose
That you could spare some bread?"
"That's quite correct," the ant replied.
"It's not that we don't care,
But just as you so rightly guessed,
We have no bread to spare.

You laughed at us this summer past,
You called us foolish drones;
But now your songs have died away,
And all we hear are groans.
We worked and saved, we saved and worked,
And now we're snug and warm,
While you may sing and you may dance
All through the winter's storm."

Remember, please, the clever ants:
First we labor; *then* we dance.

From
The Hat-Shaking Dance
and Other Ashanti Tales from Ghana

All Stories Are Anansi's

By **Harold Courlander**

with **Albert Kofi Prempeh**

Illustrated by **David Diaz**

AWARD WINNING Author/Illustrator

In the beginning, all tales and stories belonged to Nyame, the Sky God. But Kwaku Anansi, the spider, yearned to be the owner of all the stories known in the world, and he went to Nyame and offered to buy them.

The Sky God said: "I am willing to sell the stories, but the price is high. Many people have come to me offering to buy, but the price was too high for them. Rich and powerful families have not been able to pay. Do you think you can do it?"

Anansi replied to the Sky God: "I can do it. What is the price?"

"My price is three things," the Sky God said. "I must first have Mmoboro, the hornets. I must then have Onini, the great python. I must then have Osebo, the leopard. For these things I will sell you the right to tell all stories."

Anansi said: "I will bring them."

He went home and made his plans. He first cut a gourd from a vine and made a small hole in it. He took a large calabash and filled it with water. He went to the tree where the hornets lived. He poured some of the water over himself, so that he was dripping. He threw some water over the hornets, so that they too were dripping. Then he put the calabash on his head, as though to protect himself from a storm, and called out to the hornets: "Are you foolish people? Why do you stay in the rain that is falling?"

The hornets answered: "Where shall we go?"

"Go here, in this dry gourd," Anansi told them.

The hornets thanked him and flew into the gourd through the small hole. When the last of them had entered, Anansi plugged the hole with a ball of grass, saying: "Oh, yes, but you are really foolish people!"

He took his gourd full of hornets to Nyame, the Sky God. The Sky God accepted them. He said: "There are two more things."

Anansi returned to the forest and cut a long bamboo pole and some strong vines. Then he walked toward the house of Onini, the python, talking to himself. He said: "My wife is stupid. I say he is longer and stronger. My wife says he is shorter and weaker. I give him more respect. She gives him less respect. Is she right or am I right? I am right, he is longer. I am right, he is stronger."

When Onini, the python, heard Anansi talking to himself, he said: "Why are you arguing this way with yourself?"

The spider replied: "Ah, I have had a dispute with my

wife. She says you are shorter and weaker than this bamboo pole. I say you are longer and stronger."

Onini said: "It's useless and silly to argue when you can find out the truth. Bring the pole and we will measure."

So Anansi laid the pole on the ground, and the python came and stretched himself out beside it.

"You seem a little short," Anansi said.

The python stretched further.

"A little more," Anansi said.

"I can stretch no more," Onini said.

"When you stretch at one end, you get shorter at the other end," Anansi said. "Let me tie you at the front so you don't slip."

He tied Onini's head to the pole. Then he went to the other end and tied the tail to the pole. He wrapped the vine all around Onini, until the python couldn't move.

"Onini," Anansi said, "it turns out that my wife was right and I was wrong. You are shorter than the pole and weaker. My opinion wasn't as good as my wife's. But you were even more foolish than I, and you are now my prisoner."

Anansi carried the python to Nyame, the Sky God, who said: "There is one thing more."

Osebo, the leopard, was next. Anansi went into the forest and dug a deep pit where the leopard was accustomed to walk. He covered it with small branches and leaves and put dust on it, so that it was impossible to tell where the pit was. Anansi went away and hid. When Osebo came prowling in the black of night, he stepped into the trap Anansi had prepared and fell to the bottom. Anansi heard the sound of the leopard falling, and he said: "Ah, Osebo, you are half-foolish!"

When morning came, Anansi went to the pit and saw the leopard there.

"Osebo," he asked, "what are you doing in this hole?"

"I have fallen into a trap," Osebo said. "Help me out."

"I would gladly help you," Anansi said. "But I'm sure that if I bring you out, I will have no thanks for it. You will get hungry, and later on you will be wanting to eat me and my children."

"I swear it won't happen!" Osebo said.

"Very well. Since you swear it, I will take you out," Anansi said.

He bent a tall green tree toward the ground, so that its top was over the pit, and he tied it that way. Then he tied a rope to the top of the tree and dropped the other end of it into the pit.

"Tie this to your tail," he said.

Osebo tied the rope to his tail.

"Is it well tied?" Anansi asked.

"Yes, it is well tied," the leopard said.

"In that case," Anansi said, "you are not merely half-foolish, you are all-foolish."

And he took his knife and cut the other rope, the one that held the tree bowed to the ground. The tree straightened up with a snap, pulling Osebo out of the hole. He hung in the air head downward, twisting and turning. And while he hung this way, Anansi killed him with his weapons.

Then he took the body of the leopard and carried it to Nyame, the Sky God, saying: "Here is the third thing. Now I have paid the price."

Nyame said to him: "Kwaku Anansi, great warriors and chiefs have tried, but they have been unable to do it. You have done it. Therefore, I will give you the stories. From this day onward, all stories belong to you. Whenever a man tells a story, he must acknowledge that it is Anansi's tale."

In this way Anansi, the spider, became the owner of all stories that are told. To Anansi all these tales belong.

How to
Write a Fable

Over the centuries people have often told brief stories that teach a lesson or a moral. Aesop, who lived in ancient Greece, was a famous writer of these tales, which are called fables.

What is a fable? A fable is a very short story used to teach a lesson or a moral. The moral is usually stated at the end of the story. The characters in a fable are often animals that act like people. Their actions help to explain the moral or the lesson.

FABLES

ARNOLD LOBEL

● The title appears at the top of the page.

● Fables are usually short, only one or two pages.

THE CAMEL DANCES

The Camel had her heart set on becoming a ballet dancer. "To make every movement a thing of grace and beauty," said the Camel. "That is my one and only desire."

Again and again she practiced her pirouettes, her relevés, and her arabesques. She repeated the five basic positions a hundred times each day. She worked for long months under the hot desert sun. Her feet were blistered, and her body ached with fatigue, but not once did she think of stopping.

At last the Camel said, "Now I am a dancer." She announced a recital, and danced before an invited group of camel friends and critics. When her dance was over, she made a deep bow.

There was no applause.

"I must tell you frankly," said a member of the audience, "as a critic and a spokesman for this group, that you are lumpy and humpy. You are baggy and bumpy. You are, like the rest of us, simply a camel. You are *not* and never will be a ballet dancer!"

Chuckling and laughing, the audience moved away across the sand.

"How very wrong they are!" said the Camel. "I have worked hard. There can be no doubt that I am a splendid dancer. I will dance and dance just for myself."

That is what she did. It gave her many years of pleasure.

Satisfaction will come to those who please themselves.

● The moral is set off from the rest of the text.

● The moral is given at the end of the fable.

1 Choose a Moral

In order to write a fable, it is easier to choose a moral or lesson first and then plan a story around it. Think of the moral or lesson as the "punch line" of the story. One way to choose a moral or a lesson is to make a list of sayings, such as "Look before you leap" or "Haste makes waste." If you want, invent your own. After you complete your list, choose one saying that you think teaches an important lesson.

TOOLS

- paper and pencil
- colored markers

2 Plan Your Fable

Now that you have decided on your moral, it's time to plan your fable. What should happen in the story in order for your moral to make sense? Think about a beginning, a middle, and an ending for your story. Jot down some ideas for possible plots and choose the one that best illustrates the lesson you want to teach. Remember that fables are short, so you will want to keep the action simple.

Next, decide what characters will be needed. Then, think about the setting. Where will your fable take place? Keep track of your final ideas by making a chart with three columns—the first for "Characters," the second for "Setting," and the last for "Plot Summary."

3 Write Your Story

Use the ideas on your chart to write a first draft of your fable. If you are having trouble getting started, sketch the main scenes of your story. Imagine what the figures are saying to each other. Start writing your draft based on your sketches. Once you have completed a rough draft, revise it to be sure the story and the moral are clear. Be sure to use lots of descriptive language and action verbs in your writing. At the end of the fable, write your moral. Then give your fable a snappy title.

Tip A good title can often be found in a phrase from the story.

Characters	Setting	Plot Summary
a frog	pond with lily pads	A fly buzzes around a frog and brags that he is too fast for the frog to catch him. The fly is wrong.

4 Share Your Fable

If you have time, you may want to illustrate your fable. When everyone is finished, exchange fables. See if you and your classmates can guess the moral of the story before reading it at the end. Your class may want to make a book of all the fables to share with other classes.

If You Are Using a Computer ...

Create your fable in the Report format on the computer. Add clip art to illustrate your fable. Then, using the title-page maker, create a cover for your work.

THINK

Do you think fables are a good way to teach a lesson or a moral? Why or why not?

Ellen Poon
Computer Artist ▶

Stories present faraway worlds
and remarkable characters.

Fantastic Voyages

Travel to a world
created by an
artist's special
paintbrush. View
a collection of
paintings by a
surrealistic painter.

Read a story about a boy
who has an early-morning
encounter with extra-
terrestrials. Enjoy some
scenes from a
blockbuster science
fiction movie.

WORKSHOP 2

Design a movie
poster for your
own fabulous
film.

ADVENTURE COMES TO LIFE

THE INDIAN CUPBOARD

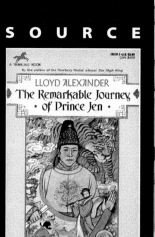

When Chen-cho, the
painter, saved the
life of a young man
dressed in rags, he
didn't expect anything
in return. But the man
insisted Chen-cho take
a sandalwood paintbox
as his reward. What
Chen-cho doesn't
know is that the poor
stranger is really a
prince, and the paint-
box isn't what it
seems, either. . .

FROM *THE REMARKABLE JOURNEY OF PRINCE JEN*

THE TALE
OF THE
TIGER'S PAINTBRUSH

BY LLOYD ALEXANDER

ILLUSTRATED BY *Chi Chung*

AWARD WINNING

Book

CHEN-CHO THE PAINTER was a good-natured, easygoing sort. He liked his food and drink, though as often as not he did without either. Not because he suffered any lack of customers. He was, in fact, a most excellent artist, and many who saw his pictures wished eagerly to buy them. To Chen-cho, however, parting with one of his landscapes was like having a tooth pulled. Sometimes, of course, he was obliged to do so, when he needed a few strings of cash to keep body and soul together—although usually he spent the money on paper and paint. On the other hand, out of sudden impulse or foolish whim, he was just as likely to give away one of his pictures to a passerby who wistfully admired but could ill afford to purchase it.

For the rest, he was a little absentminded, his head so filled with colors and shapes that he lost track of time, forgot to wash his face or change his clothes. With his collapsing umbrella, his felt cap, his bespattered trousers flapping around his ankles, he became a familiar sight in towns and villages where he stopped in the course of his wanderings. Children tagged after him, fascinated to peer over his shoulder as he worked. Local officials, however, felt more comfortable after he left.

Now, with the sandalwood box on the table in front of him, paying no attention to the rejoicing villagers crowding the inn, Chen-cho gleefully scrutinized his gift. As an artist, he had immediately recognized the excellence of the materials, but he studied them again to confirm his first opinion.

He picked up the stick of black ink and rolled it around in his fingers. He sniffed at it, even tasted it, and licked his lips as if it were some delicious morsel.

"Marvelous!" Chen-cho said to himself. "Perfect! No question, this ink's made from the ashes of pine trees on the south slope of Mount Lu, the very best."

Next, he turned his attention to the ink stone, with its shallow little basin for water at one end and its flat surface for grinding the solid ink at the other. The stone was fine-grained, flawless; and, in color, an unusual reddish gray. Chen-cho rubbed his thumb over it lovingly and shook his head in amazement.

"Here's a treasure in itself! I've heard of stones like this. They come only from one place: a grotto in Mount Wu-shan. I never believed they were more than legend. Yet, I have one right in my hand."

Chuckling over his good fortune, blessing the stranger he had fondly nicknamed Honorable Ragbag, the painter picked up the last object in the box: a paintbrush with a long bamboo handle.

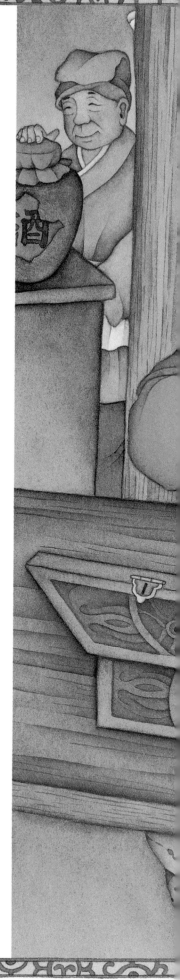

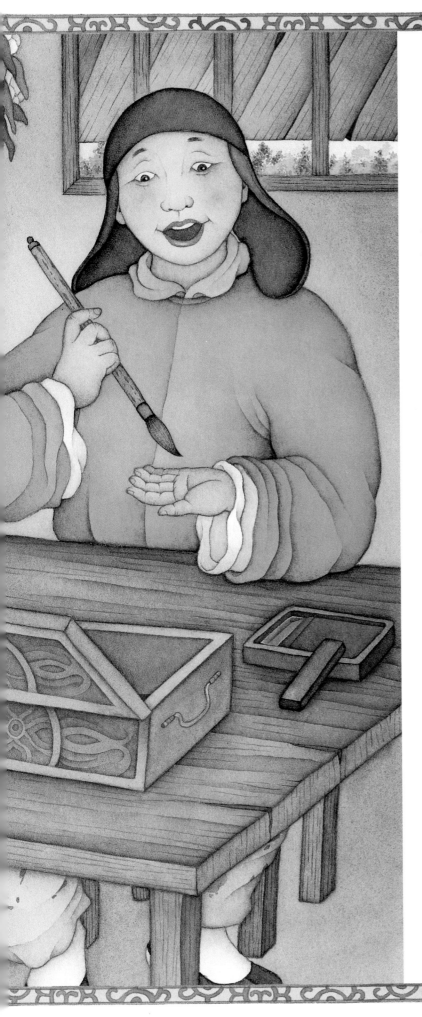

"This is odd." Chen-cho squinted at the brush hairs, tested them on the palm of his hand and the tip of his nose. "Soft? Firm? Both at once? What's it made of? Not rabbit fur, not wolf hair, not mouse whiskers."

The painter could not restrain himself another moment. He called the landlord for a cup of water, poured a little into the basin of the ink stone, then carefully rubbed the tip of the ink stick against the grinding surface. No matter how much he rubbed, the stick showed no trace of wear.

"At this rate," he said to himself, "it will last forever. One stick, and ink enough for the rest of my life. There's frugality for you!"

He pulled out a sheet of paper. Moistening the brush, rolling the tip in the ink he had ground, he made a couple of trial strokes. As he did, a thrill began at the tip of his toes, raced to his arm, his hand, his fingers. The sensation turned him giddy. He glanced at the paper. His jaw dropped. The brush strokes were not black. They were bright vermilion.

"I'd have sworn that ink was black," Chen-cho murmured. "Was I mistaken? Yes, no doubt. The light's dim here."

He made a few more brush strokes. They were no longer vermilion, but jade green. Chen-cho put down the brush and rubbed his chin.

"What's happening here? That ink stick's black as night, through and through. What's doing it? The stone? The brush? No matter, let's have another go."

Chen-cho daubed at the paper, which was soon covered with streaks of bright orange, red, and blue. Anyone else might have grown alarmed or frightened at such an uncanny happening. But Chen-cho enjoyed surprises, mysteries, and extraordinary events. And so he laughed with delight to find himself owner of these remarkable materials.

"Well, old fellow," he said to himself, "you've come onto something you never expected and probably better than you deserve. Let's try something else. Those are marvelous colors, but what if I wanted a sort of lilac purple-green with a reddish cast?"

No sooner did Chen-cho imagine such a hue than it flowed from his brush. He quickly discovered that he need only envision whatever shade he wanted, and there it was, from brush to paper.

"That's what I call convenient and efficient," exclaimed the joyous Chen-cho. "No more paint pots and a dozen different pigments. Here's everything all at once."

With that, he clapped his felt hat firmly on his head, seized a handful of papers, packed up the box, and hurried out of the inn. He ran all the way to the stream where he had first met Ragbag. There he settled himself, ignoring the weather, forgetting to put up his umbrella, and worked away happily, letting the brush go as it wished, hardly glancing at what he was doing.

It was dusk and the light had faded before he could make himself leave off. But the picture was finished, better than anything he had ever painted. Chen-cho laughed and slapped his leg. "Old boy," he told himself, "keep on like this and you might even do something worthwhile."

He went back to his room at the inn. Excited by his wonderful new possessions, he forgot to eat his dinner. He barely slept that night, eager to start another picture.

Next morning and for several days thereafter, Chen-cho went into the countryside looking for scenes to paint. Each landscape that took shape under his hand delighted him more than the one before.

It snowed heavily on a certain morning. Chen-cho usually paid no mind to bad weather. That day, the wind blew so sharply and the snow piled up so deeply that he decided to stay in his room. Nevertheless, his fingers itched to take up the brush. Ordinarily, he painted outdoors, according to whatever vista caught his eye. This time, he thought to do something else.

"Why not make up my own landscape? I'll paint whatever pops into my head and strikes my fancy."

Taking one of his largest sheets of paper, he set about painting hills and valleys, forests and streams, adding glens and lakes wherever it pleased him. He painted rolling meadows he had never seen; and bright banks of flowers he invented as he went along; and clouds of fantastic shapes, all drenched in sunlight, with a couple of rainbows added for good measure.

"What this may be, I've no idea," Chen-cho said when he finished. He blinked happily at the picture. "All I know is: I've astonished myself. That's something that never happened before."

Chen-cho could not take his eyes from his handiwork. He peered at it from every angle, first from a distance, then so close he bumped his nose.

"If I didn't know better," he said, "I'd swear I could smell those flowers. In fact, if I hadn't painted them, I'd believe I could pick one."

He reached out, pretending to pluck a blossom. Next thing he knew, the flower lay in his hand.

Chen-cho gaped at it. He swallowed hard, then grinned and shook his head. "What you've done, you foolish fellow, is go to sleep on your feet. You're having a dream. A marvelous one, but that's all it is."

He pinched himself, rubbed his eyes, soaked his head in a basin of water, paced back and forth. The flower was still where he had set it on the table. Fragrance filled the room.

"I'm wide-awake, no question about it," he finally admitted. He went again to the picture. "That being the case, let's examine this reasonably. It seems I've put my hand into it. What, for example, if I did—this?"

Chen-cho poked his head into the painted landscape. Indeed, he could look around him at the trees and lakes. The sunshine dazzled and warmed him. He sniffed the fragrant air. He heard the rush of a waterfall somewhere in the distance.

"This is definitely out of the ordinary," Chen-cho murmured, pulling back his head. "Dare I explore a little farther?"

With that, Chen-cho plucked up his courage and stepped all the way into the picture.

He was not certain how he did it. The painting was large, but far from as large as the artist himself. Yet, it must have grown spacious enough to take him in, for there he was, standing knee-deep in the soft grass of a meadow.

"So far so good," he said. "But now I've gone in—how do I get out?"

He answered his own question by easily stepping back into the room. His first apprehension gave way to delight as he discovered that he could walk in and out of the painting as often as he pleased.

With each venture into the landscape, Chen-cho found himself becoming all the more comfortable and confident.

"It's quite amazing, hard to believe," Chen-cho remarked. "But I suppose one can get used to anything, including miracles."

A fascinating thought sprang to mind. What, he wondered, lay beyond the fields and forests and across the valleys?

"I've no idea what's there," he said, "which is the best reason to go and find out."

Chen-cho picked up the sandalwood box and a sheaf of paper in case he found some especially attractive scene. Stepping into the landscape, he set off eagerly along a gentle path that opened at his feet. He soon came to a high-arched bridge over a stream lined with willows. The view so charmed him that he spread his paper and began to paint.

He stopped in the middle of a brush stroke. He had the impression of being watched. When he turned around, he saw that his impression was correct.

Sitting on its haunches, observing him through a pair of orange eyes, was an enormous tiger.

"Hello there, Chen-cho." The tiger padded toward him, stripes rippling at every fluid pace. "My name is Lao-hu. I've been expecting you."

"A pleasure to make your acquaintance," replied Chen-cho. Having by now grown accustomed to marvelous happenings, the arrival of a tiger did not unsettle him too much, especially since the big animal had addressed him in a friendly tone. "However, I can't truthfully say I was expecting you."

"You must have, whether you knew it or not," Lao-hu said. "Otherwise, I wouldn't be here. Ah. I see you've been using my brush."

"Yours?"

"My hairs," Lao-hu said. "From the tip of my tail. I hope it pleases you."

"A remarkable brush," Chen-cho said. "I'd go so far as to call it miraculous. From the tip of your tail? Yes, but in that case, I'm a little puzzled. I hope you don't mind my asking, but if you weren't here until I painted this picture, where were you before I painted it? If you were someplace else, how did you get here? And who plucked out those hairs in the first place?"

"Why concern yourself with details?" Lao-hu yawned enormously. "It's a tedious, boring matter you wouldn't understand to begin with. Let me just say this: You're not the first to paint such a picture, nor the last. Many have done still finer work. And you're certainly not the first to use my brush."

"Tell me, then," Chen-cho said, "can others find their way into my picture? A question of privacy, you understand."

"Of course they can," replied Lao-hu. "It's your painting, but now that you've done it, it's open to anybody who cares to enter. But leave that idle speculation and nit-picking to scholars who enjoy such occupation. You've hardly seen the smallest part of all this"—Lao-hu motioned around him with his long tail—"so let me show you a little, for a start. Climb on my back."

Chen-cho gladly accepted the tiger's invitation. Lao-hu sprang across the stream in one mighty leap. Chen-cho clamped his legs around the tiger's flanks and his arms around Lao-hu's powerful neck. The tiger sped across meadows, through forests, up and down hills. Chen-cho glimpsed garden pavilions, farmhouses, towns and villages, sailboats on rivers, birds in the air, fish leaping in brooks, animals of every kind. Some of what he saw looked vaguely familiar; the rest, altogether strange and fascinating. Lao-hu promised they would continue their explorations and carried the painter back to where they had started.

As easily as he had stepped into the painting, Chen-cho stepped into the room. Lao-hu followed, much to the surprise and delight of the painter, who was reluctant to part from his new companion.

"I can go wherever I please," Lao-hu replied when Chen-cho asked about this, "just as you can."

"Can other people see you?" asked Chen-cho, wondering what his landlord might say if he came into the room and found a tiger.

"Of course they can," Lao-hu said. "I may be a magical tiger, but I'm not an invisible one."

With that, Lao-hu curled up at the foot of Chen-cho's bed. The tired but happy painter flung himself down and went to sleep, thinking that, all in all, it had been an interesting day.

Next morning, when the storm had passed, Chen-cho packed his belongings and set off on his way again. Lao-hu had jumped back into the picture, which the artist had rolled up and carried under his arm. Once away from the village, Chen-cho unrolled the painting. He saw no sign of Lao-hu. Dismayed, the artist anxiously called for him. The tiger appeared an instant later, sprang out, and padded along beside Chen-cho.

From then on, whenever he was sure they were unobserved, Chen-cho summoned Lao-hu, and the two of them wandered together, the fondest companions. When Chen-cho stopped to paint some scene or other, the tiger would stretch out next to him or disappear into the picture on some business of his own. Nevertheless, Chen-cho had only to call his name and Lao-hu would reappear immediately; and Chen-cho always kept the painting beside him when he worked.

As for his other paintings, thanks to the tiger's brush, the marvelous ink stick, and the grinding stone they became better and better, as did Chen-cho's reputation. Whenever he lodged in a town or city, he could expect any number of customers to come clamoring for his pictures. However, as always, he parted with few. Nor would he even consider selling his marvelous landscape, no matter what price was offered. So, more often than not, would-be purchasers left disappointed at being refused.

Only once did Chen-cho have a disagreeable encounter. In one town, a merchant came to inspect Chen-cho's paintings, but as soon as he saw them, he shook his head in distaste.

"What dreadful daubs are these?" he exclaimed. "Not one suitable to put in my house! And this"—he pointed at the landscape, where Lao-hu had prudently hidden himself out of sight—"worst of all! An ugly, blotchy, ill-conceived scrawl! I've had nightmares prettier than this."

Chen-cho, glad to see the merchant stamp off, flung a few tart words after him. He was, nonetheless, puzzled. He called Lao-hu, who popped out instantly.

"Easily understood," Lao-hu said, when Chen-cho told him the merchant's opinion. "As a painter, you should know this better than anyone. We see with eyes in our head, but see clearer with eyes of the heart. Some see beauty, some see ugliness. In both cases, what they see is a reflection of their own nature."

"Even so," replied Chen-cho, "a painting's a painting. Colors and shapes don't change, no matter who looks at them."

"True enough," said Lao-hu. "Very well, then, let me put it this way: You can't please everybody."

"That, I suppose," Chen-cho said, "is a blessing."

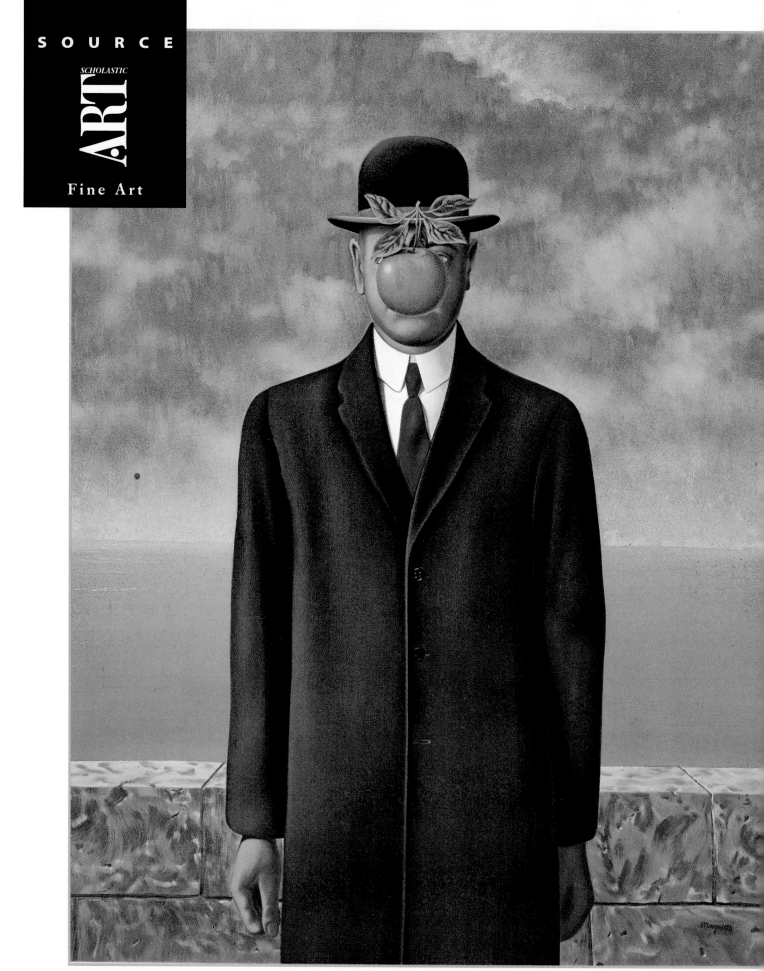

The Son of Man, 1964. Oil on canvas. Private Collection. NY,NY.

THE STRANGE WORLDS OF

René Magritte

A man in a black suit and hat stands against an ordinary stone wall below a bright blue sky. The painting technique is very realistic, the figure is very solid, and the wall looks very real. There is only one element that keeps this painting from being not only realistic, but quite boring. There is a bright green apple over the man's face. What is it doing there? Why doesn't he notice it? What does it mean? Is it supposed to be funny, sinister, or both?

Everything is absurd in the world of Belgian painter René Magritte. Trains scream out of fireplaces, paintings turn into windows, and stone castles rise high above the ocean. Magritte doesn't exaggerate or distort his subjects to achieve these shocking effects. He paints almost photographically, except that he juxtaposes (places side by side) objects that don't belong together. Sometimes he will change only one thing, but that change is so significant that the resulting image is unforgettable.

Look at these images carefully. What has Magritte done in each painting to turn the believable into the bizarre?

The Chateau in the Pyrenees, 1959. The Israel Museum, Jerusalem.

Time Transfixed, 1938. Oil on canvas. Joseph Winterbotham Collection.

From **Bruce Coville's**
Book of Aliens

How I Maybe

SAVED

By
Lawrence
Watt-Evans

Illustrated by Jenny Adams

THE WORLD

Last Tuesday Before Breakfast

When I woke up last Tuesday morning and found out that it was only six-fifteen and my kid sister Karen was tugging at my sleeve, I was really mad. She wasn't supposed to be in my room *ever*, and especially not when I was trying to sleep.

"What do *you* want?" I growled.

"Craig, you gotta come downstairs *right now*," she said, not loud, but talking right into my ear.

"No, I don't," I told her, and I pulled the blankets up over my head.

"Yes, you *do*," she said. "You've gotta come and see what I found.

You've gotta help me talk Mom and Dad into letting me keep it."

I blinked under the covers.

Keep it? Keep *what*?

I decided that maybe I'd better get up after all. Karen's six, just half my age, but she gets into twice as much trouble. This sounded as if it might be even more trouble than usual.

"Go away and let me get dressed," I said.

When I heard the door close, I got out of bed and threw on my jeans and a T-shirt as fast as I could. Then I went downstairs, and there was Karen, waiting in the front hall.

"Come on," she said, opening the front door.

"*Karen*," I said, "you aren't supposed to go out before Mom and Dad get up!"

"Just to the porch!" she said.

Well, that was probably okay, and anyway, she was outside before I could argue any more, so I followed her.

"Karen, what is this all…" Then I stopped and stared.

She had it under the old laundry basket Mom had given her to keep toys in, and I couldn't see it very well, but I could see that it was moving, and that it was purple. Not a dull purple like maybe a lizard would be, but a really *bright* purple. I knelt on the porch and took a look through the plastic mesh.

It was furry and purple all over. It had six legs, and big yellow-green eyes, and some wiggly things that weren't exactly tentacles, but that was the closest thing I could think of. It was looking back at me.

It sounds scary, but it wasn't. It was really cute. I wasn't really all the way awake yet, so I wasn't thinking very clearly, but I still knew there just *isn't* anything with six legs and purple fur, either cute *or* scary. My eyes got big as I stared at it, trying to figure it out, and it stared back.

"I'm gonna keep it," Karen said. "I'm gonna name it Roger."

"Karen, you *can't* keep it," I said. "We don't know what it *is*."

"It's *mine*," Karen said.

"Where'd you find it?"

"Here on the porch," she said, but she said it with the "you better believe this" tone that means she's telling a whopper. I decided not to argue about that.

"Well, you can't keep it. We don't know what it is, or where it came from, or anything. Maybe somebody's looking for it."

She got a stubborn look on her face. "Nobody's looking for Roger," she said. "If anyone around here had a pet like that, we'd have heard about it. Remember when Mr. Bester had that snake, and all the neighbors

tried to make him get rid of it?"

"It's not the same thing," I said, but she was sort of right. I couldn't imagine how anyone could have had a thing like that without everyone in the neighborhood knowing about it.

In fact, I didn't think anyone could have a thing like that without everyone in the *world* knowing about it. *Purple* fur? *Six* legs?

I looked at the thing again, and it made a squeaky little noise.

I knew we couldn't keep it, whatever it was—Mom wouldn't even let us have a cat. I wasn't sure what to do about it, though. If we just turned it loose, it might get hurt. We didn't know where it came from, or anything.

But then I got to thinking about where it *could* have come from, and I could feel my eyes get even bigger. Even though it was the middle of July and the morning was already sunny and warm, I suddenly felt kind of cold.

"Karen," I said, "where'd you *really* find it?"

She just looked at me stubbornly.

"C'mon, you've gotta tell me!"

"Why?" she demanded, sticking out her chin.

"Because I think it must have come from outer space," I explained.

Then *her* eyes got big.

"Maybe they're going to invade us!" I said.

"What's 'invade'?"

"Try to take over and make everybody slaves. Like a war, kind of, only worse."

She looked at me as if I'd just said something really stupid. "*Roger* wouldn't hurt anybody," she said, pointing at the laundry basket.

I looked at Roger, and he blinked at me and made a sort of "Eep!" noise.

I had to admit he wasn't exactly a scary monster from outer space; he wasn't any bigger than Ms. Watson's cat Sugarplum, and I didn't see any fangs or claws or anything. And those tentacle things didn't look dangerous.

But if he wasn't a monster from outer space, what the heck *was* he?

"Well, maybe Roger's one of their slaves that got away," I said. "Maybe he's trying to warn us."

"He doesn't talk."

"He doesn't talk *English*," I corrected her. "Come on, we've gotta let him out of there."

"No!" she said. "If you let him out, Craig, I'll never speak to you again, and I'll go into your room and wreck all your stuff!"

"But, Karen," I said, "he's a monster from outer space!"

"He is *not*!"

"You don't know what he is!"

"Neither do you!"

Well, that was true. I couldn't think of much of anything he could be *except* a monster from outer space, but maybe he was some kind of mutant or something, instead.

"C'mon, Karen, where'd you really find him? If you don't tell me, I *will* let him go." I grabbed the laundry basket as if I was going to lift it and let Roger out.

"Don't you dare!" she said, and she fell forward on top of the basket, holding it down. I was afraid for a second she was going to squash it, and Roger with it, but she doesn't weigh much, and the basket held up.

"Then tell me where you found him!" If I had to, I could pick up her *and* the basket, and she knew it.

"Promise you won't tell?"

I hate making promises like that, but I said, "Okay, I promise."

"Down by the lake."

I stared at her.

We live out at the edge of town, where the land starts getting hilly and woodsy, and if you go down to the end of the street and cut through Billy Wechsler's back yard, you can get into a state park, and right up to the edge of a big lake—Lake Cohoptick, it's called. We aren't allowed to go there without a grown-up along, ever since a kid almost drowned there when

Karen was just a baby.

"You went down to the *lake*?" I said. I tried to think of some way out of my promise not to tell Mom, because even though Karen's a real pain sometimes, I didn't want her to get herself killed. And besides, if Mom found out that Karen went there, and that I knew about it and didn't tell, *I'd* be in trouble. I'm the older one; I'm supposed to be responsible.

Karen must have figured out what I was thinking. "You promised!" she yelled.

"I know I did," I said. "Do you… I mean, is this the first time?"

She nodded. "There were these funny lights, and I wanted to see what they were."

"What were they?"

"I don't know. They were gone by the time I got there."

"But you found Roger there?"

She nodded again.

"Don't you see, silly? Those lights must have been the invaders' spaceship!" She looked at Roger, and he squeaked again. "You think he was the invaders' pet, and he escaped and ran off?"

"Maybe," I said. I looked at Roger, and he looked back at me.

"You really think they were invaders?"

"Maybe," I said again. I didn't really know what to think. I frowned, thinking hard.

"Listen, Karen," I said. "Can you show me where you found Roger? Maybe there's, you know, stuff to see there."

"We're not allowed down by the lake," she said doubtfully.

"You already went once," I pointed out.

It took me a few minutes to convince her, and I had to threaten to tell Mom and Dad about a lot of stuff, but at last she agreed. We put Roger in a box and took him along.

The hard part was sneaking through Billy Wechsler's yard, because Mrs. Wechsler was awake and getting breakfast. We saw her through the kitchen window.

Anyway, we got down near the lake, where there's a bunch of cattails and stuff, and some trees, and we were looking around when Karen tugged at my shirt and said, "Look!"

I looked where she was pointing, past some big bushes, and I started shivering and felt cold all over. I got bumps on my arms, the kind my dad calls gooseflesh, and I stood there frozen. I've never been so scared.

There were monsters walking along beside the lake.

Roger squeaked again, and I ducked down behind the cattails, holding the box shut. Karen crouched down beside me, and we watched the monsters.

There were two of them, with long bony legs and big glaring green eyes. They were purple, like Roger, only a little darker, but they were *big*, eight or nine feet tall, and they weren't cute at all. They were scary. They were stalking around on those great big legs like giant spiders, making hooting noises.

Karen started crying. "Those are the space invaders!"

"Hush!" I told her. I was afraid I'd start crying, too, if she didn't shut up. And I was even more scared that the monsters would hear.

"I bet they were gonna eat him!" she said.

"Well, shut up, or they still might!" I said. Roger would be just about the right size for a snack for those things, I thought, and I wished she hadn't suggested it.

She didn't say anything more, but she kept crying, only she was quiet about it.

I looked through the cattails and watched the monsters. They were walking back and forth, waving these long ropy things and hooting, and I supposed the hooting must be the way they talked, but it didn't sound like a language, not even like Chinese or anything, because it just seemed like the same sound over and over. They were looking down at the ground, and tramping along slowly and carefully.

I realized they were looking for Roger, and I figured they didn't want to leave any evidence around that would show they'd been there. Roger would be pretty good evidence of *something,* anyway. I thought about sneaking back up to the street and calling the police or somebody. I was pretty sure we could make it, but I didn't want to rush it. I didn't know how fast the monsters were. They were moving away, little by little, so the longer we waited, the safer we'd be.

Besides, I wanted to make sure I knew what they looked like so I could describe them.

They were purple and hairy; the bodies weren't actually much bigger than I am, but those six long long legs made them look huge. They had shiny white fangs, and these two ropy things.

And they kept hooting the exact same thing, over and over.

I frowned. I was thinking hard. I looked at the monsters, then down at the box.

"They look like Roger," I said.

"No, they don't," Karen said. "They're big and bony and horrible."

"But they've got the same number of legs and everything," I said. "And they're purple."

"So what?" she said.

"So I want to try something."

This was about the hardest thing I ever did in my life. I was still scared stiff, but I was pretty sure I had figured out something really important—what Roger was and why they were looking for him. And if I was right, then I had to do it. It would be wrong not to.

And if I was wrong, we might all be dead, but my dad always says you have to do your best and then stick to your guns, not let anyone change your mind for you.

It was the hooting that convinced me. I stood up and called, "Over here!"

Karen screamed and started pulling on my arm.

The monsters turned around to look at me, and I thought they were about to run away—one of them even *started* running, a little, all those legs tangling together like some kind of complicated mixing machine. That was when I knew for sure that they weren't invaders from outer space; real invaders wouldn't have run. Real invaders would have zapped me somehow.

But then I held up the box, and Roger stuck his head out and squeaked.

The two monsters hooted in unison, that same hoot they'd been doing before, which I had decided must be Roger's real name. Then they *both* started running.

They were running *toward* us.

They hooted a lot as they ran, not just the same thing this time, but lots of different stuff. I don't know if they were talking to each other, or thanking me, or telling Roger how glad they were to see him, or telling him how much trouble he was in for running off, but they sure hooted a lot.

Karen was scrunched into a ball at my feet, screaming, but they didn't

pay any attention to her; they ran up and snatched Roger out of the box and gave him the biggest hug I ever saw, using all four of those ropy things. Roger was squealing and squeaking like crazy. He looked really happy.

One of them untangled a ropy thing long enough to pat me on the head and hoot something very slowly at me. I said, "You're welcome."

Then the two monsters marched off, holding Roger between them.

Karen had finally quieted down, but she was still curled up on the ground with her hands over her eyes.

"Come on, silly," I told her. "You're missing it." I poked her with my toe.

She uncurled and sat up, and looked in time to see the water of the lake open up like a cellar door, and Roger and the monsters march down into the opening. Just before they were out of sight, one of them waved to me, and I waved back.

"They're gonna *eat* him!" Karen shrieked. She whacked me on the leg.

"No, they aren't," I said. "He's their *baby,* silly."

She got up slowly. "But he's so cute, and they're *ugly*!" she said.

I shrugged. "Babies are always cuter than grown-ups. Like kittens or puppies."

"But…aren't they invaders from outer space?" she asked.

I'd thought of that, when I was deciding whether to call to them. "Karen, do soldiers take their kids along when they're going to fight a war?"

Before she could answer, the ground started shaking, and we both fell down. A few minutes later there was this huge splash, and this gigantic big round *thing* came flying up out of the lake and went roaring off into the sky, lights flashing.

The lake water sprayed everywhere. We got soaked.

The spaceship, or whatever it was, took off, and we sat there dripping wet, watching it go, and Karen said, "Wow! It looks big enough to blow up the whole world!"

I nodded. It really did.

Now, probably it wouldn't have done anything anyway, because you wouldn't bring a baby along if you were going to go around blowing up planets, would you? But if they hadn't found Roger . . .

Well, maybe I saved the world last Tuesday.

But all I got out of it was grounded for a week, because Mom and Dad were up when we got home, and they were really mad when we came in dripping wet. And Karen's still sort of mad that I gave Roger back.

You know, one thing I still wonder about—after the spaceship took off, the lake looked half-empty. The water level was at least five or six feet lower. I mean, it was a *big* spaceship. So where'd all the water go when it first landed?

I guess I'll never know.

I don't care much, really; I'm just glad we're all okay and all together.

And so are Roger and his folks.

FROM

E.T.

In 1982, the movie *E.T.: The Extra-Terrestrial* hit the screen and was an instant success. Directed by Steven Spielberg and written by Melissa Mathison, *E.T.* is the story of a lonely young boy, Elliott, who finds a creature from another planet. With E.T., Elliott discovers adventures beyond his wildest imagination.

Curious about who's who in the movie?
Then check out the cast list:

ELLIOTT: A ten-year-old boy who is friendless and fatherless. He is a dreamer who finds a creature from outer space.

E.T.: The Extra-Terrestrial. A creature from outer space who is stranded on Earth when his spaceship leaves without him.

MICHAEL: Elliott's older brother. He is a typical 14-year-old boy who thinks that he knows everything.

GERTIE: Elliott's younger sister. She is a five-year-old tomboy who is wise for her age.

MARY: Elliott's mother. She's in her late thirties and really loves her kids.

HARVEY: The family dog.

Stop the cameras!

Before you start to read a movie script, you have to be familiar with the words and symbols marked on the script. Here are some directing terms to help you through.

CAMERA CUES

The numbers on the side of the script stand for the different scenes. An *A* or *X* after the number means that the scene was added or is an extra.

Back To: The camera goes back to a previous location. Imagine Gertie at the top of the stairs. The camera leaves her to go into another room. If it returns to her at the top of the stairs the camera goes "back to" Gertie.

*: Background music is shown with an asterisk (*).

Close: This means that the camera is close up. Picture the camera focusing only on E.T.'s face. Now the camera is "close."

Ext.: Exterior. The scene takes place outside.

Int.: Interior. The scene takes place inside.

O.C.: Off-camera. If you hear Elliott speaking but can't see him, he is "O.C."

POV: Point of View. Refers to the direction the camera is focusing. If Elliott is looking at E.T., then "His POV" means that the camera is looking at E.T. through his eyes.

Reverse Angle: (Reverse) This means that first the camera looks at one side of an object and then the opposite side. If the camera is looking at E.T.'s front, the "reverse angle" is looking at his back.

Wider: The camera angle becomes wider. If the camera is focusing just on E.T., and then it focuses on E.T. and Elliott next to each other, the angle has become "wider."

And now for some scenes from the movie. Action!

108   INT. ELLIOTT'S ROOM — DAY   108

MICHAEL opens the door. **ELLIOTT** stands in the center of his debris-strewn room. **MICHAEL** makes himself at home. **ELLIOTT** remains stiff and motionless.

> **MICHAEL**
> How you feeling, faker?

> **ELLIOTT**
> Fine.

> **MICHAEL**
> Tyler said he got sixty-nine thousand at Asteroids yesterday, but he pulled the plug so, who knows . . .

> **ELLIOTT**
> I've got something really important to tell you.

MICHAEL looks up

> **ELLIOTT**
> Okay. This is the most important, probably the most serious thing ever.

> **MICHAEL**
> What'd you do?

> **ELLIOTT**
> Okay. Remember the goblin?

> **MICHAEL**
> You're so lame, Elliott.

> **ELLIOTT**
> He came back.

> **MICHAEL**
> Right!

> **ELLIOTT**
> One thing, I have absolute power. Say it.

> **MICHAEL**
> What have you got? Is it the coyote? Let me see it!

> **ELLIOTT**
> No. Swear first. The most excellent promise you can make.

MICHAEL
Okay. Okay. He's yours.
Mom's going to kill you.

ELLIOTT
Okay. Stand over there. And
you'd better take off your
shoulder pads.

MICHAEL
What!

ELLIOTT
You might scare him. Go on.

**MICHAEL removes his shoulder pads as
ELLIOTT goes to the closet.**

ELLIOTT
(O.C.) And close your eyes!

MICHAEL
Don't push it.

ELLIOTT
(O.C.) I'm not coming out until
your eyes are closed.

MICHAEL
Okay, they're closed.

**ELLIOTT and E.T. step out of the closet.
ELLIOTT puts his arm over E.T.'s shoulder and
nods to the creature reassuringly. He looks at his
brother again.**

ELLIOTT
Swear it, one more time, I have…

MICHAEL
You have absolute power, all right
already.

The door suddenly flies open.

**GERTIE comes running in. She sees E.T. and lets
out a terrified scream. MICHAEL opens his eyes,
sees E.T. and screams. E.T. screams. ELLIOTT
screams. ELLIOTT catches himself and yells.**

ELLIOTT
Make her stop!

**MICHAEL clamps his hand over Gertie's mouth.
GERTIE clutches her three-foot Indian doll.**

ELLIOTT
In the closet. Fast.

MICHAEL hurries GERTIE into the closet.

109   INT. CLOSET — DAY   109
MICHAEL and GERTIE leap into the closet. The door closes, then opens a second later, and E.T. comes tumbling into the closet. The door closes with a bang.

110   INT. ELLIOTT'S ROOM — DAY   110
MARY steps into ELLIOTT's room. ELLIOTT is draped over the stuffed chair. The room looks as if a cyclone hit it.

MARY
Hi, honey…what happened in here!

ELLIOTT
What do you mean?

MARY
Look at this! How is this possible?

111   INT. CLOSET — DAY   111
MICHAEL still has his hand over GERTIE's mouth. Both children have their eyes glued on E.T. E.T. turns from the children's fearful faces to peek between the slats of the louvered door.

112   HIS POV: MARY   112
ELLIOTT
Oh. You mean my room.

MARY
This isn't a room. This is an accident.

MARY walks across the room and kisses ELLIOTT on the forehead.

113   INT. ELLIOTT'S ROOM — DAY   113

ELLIOTT
I'll clean it.

MARY
This must mean that you're feeling well enough to go to school tomorrow.

ELLIOTT nods. MARY heads for the door.

MARY
You fellas keep an eye on Gertie while I take a shower.

ELLIOTT

For sure.

MARY leaves.

You could cut the silence with a knife.
ELLIOTT enters. The children speak in whispers.

MICHAEL

Elliott?

ELLIOTT

I'm keeping him!

MICHAEL

You gotta tell Mom.

ELLIOTT

She'll want to do the right thing. You
know what that means, don't you?
(points to E.T.) Dog food. Or lobotomy.

MICHAEL

What is it?

ELLIOTT

He's good. I can feel it.

MICHAEL indicates GERTIE

MICHAEL

She'll blab it for sure.

ELLIOTT

Gertie, he's not going to hurt you.

ELLIOTT smiles. GERTIE nods. MICHAEL loosens
his grip.

GERTIE

Is he a boy or a girl?

ELLIOTT

Ah . . . he's a boy.

GERTIE

How can you tell?

ELLIOTT

Now you're not going to tell, are you?
Even Mom?

GERTIE

Why not?

Because, ah, grown-ups can't see
him. Only kids can see him.

ELLIOTT looks at MICHAEL.

ELLIOTT
You know what will happen if you tell?

**MICHAEL takes GERTIE's Indian doll and pretends he
is wrenching its arm off.**

ELLIOTT
Do it, Mike. We have to.

MICHAEL
(in a Mr. Bill voice)
No. No! Don't break my arm, please! I'll
do anything, it hurts, please!

GERTIE's eyes fill with terror. E.T. watches.

GERTIE
Stop! Stop it!

ELLIOTT
Promise?

GERTIE
Yes.

ELLIOTT
For sure?

MICHAEL and GERTIE nod.

GERTIE
Is he from the moon?

MICHAEL
Was he wearing any clothes?

ELLIOTT
Nope. Yeah, he's from the moon. Isn't
that exciting?

GERTIE nods.

MARY
(O.C.) Come help with dinner.
Everybody!

ELLIOTT smiles at E.T. then nods to the others.

ELLIOTT
Okay. Act straight.

The family sits at the dinner table nibbling the remains of their hamburgers, each lost in his or her own thoughts.

ELLIOTT wipes his mouth.

> ELLIOTT
>
> Delicious.

ELLIOTT gets up with his plate.

> ELLIOTT
>
> (to **MARY**)
>
> May I take your plate?

> MARY
>
> Yes, thank you.

MARY is amused by **ELLIOTT's** manners. **ELLIOTT** takes the plates to the sink.

> ELLIOTT
>
> I made a house in the big closet today.

MICHAEL suddenly rises with his plate and carries it to the sink. He gives **ELLIOTT** a quick hip-shot.

> MARY
>
> What kind of house?

> ELLIOTT
>
> Sort of like a hideout.

> GERTIE
>
> Mama, why do we see what you don't see?

> MICHAEL
>
> We don't.

> MARY
>
> (to **GERTIE**)
>
> Because we're different people, we see things differently.
>
> (to **ELLIOTT**)
>
> What did you do with all the stuff that was in there?

> ELLIOTT
>
> I reorganized.

MARY

Oh, really?

GERTIE

What are the people who aren't people?

MICHAEL

There's no such thing.

MARY puts the kettle on the stove.

ELLIOTT

Can I keep the hideout?

GERTIE

Can he?

MARY

For a little while.

MARY goes to the cupboard for the teapot.

MARY

Too bad I won't be able to see it until
Elliott cleans his room.

**While her back is turned, the children share a
victorious moment.**

GERTIE

(whispers to ELLIOTT)

She really can't see it?

MARY fills the teapot.

MARY

I've got stuff to do. Will you finish up in
here?

MICHAEL

Absolutely.

**The children all smile at MARY as she leaves the room.
The moment she is gone, ELLIOTT grabs a clean plate,
and each child adds some tidbit of food to E.T.'s dinner.
ELLIOTT heads for the hallway with a tray full of food.**

ELLIOTT

Watch her. When the coast is clear, you
can come in. Knock three times.

116   **INT. SECOND FLOOR HALLWAY — NIGHT 116**
**MICHAEL sneaks up the stairs, taps three times at
ELLIOTT's door and is granted passage. GERTIE is
right behind him.**

MARY is sitting on the floor of her bedroom folding laundry. She looks up and sees GERTIE.

> MARY
>
> What are you doing, Gertie?

> GERTIE
>
> I'm going to play in Elliott's room.

> MARY
>
> Okay. Don't let them torture you.

GERTIE pauses at the top of the stairway, lifts a rather droopy geranium in a pot and carries it to ELLIOTT's door.

MICHAEL lets GERTIE in. HARVEY butts his way in behind her. E.T. immediately notices the geranium in GERTIE's hands. He eats an orange without peeling it. The children speak to one another in whispers.

> MICHAEL
>
> Maybe he's just some animal that wasn't supposed to live. You know, like those rabbits we saw that time.

> ELLIOTT
>
> Don't be lame.

> MICHAEL
>
> But I don't believe in stuff like this.

> ELLIOTT
>
> I do. Now. I always did, really.

E.T. examines some clay on ELLIOTT's desk. He closes his fingers, and the clay gushes through them.

> ELLIOTT
>
> I got an idea, get the atlas.

MICHAEL pulls the atlas from ELLIOTT's shelf. They open it, lay it across E.T.'s plate and turn pages until they reach the United States.

> ELLIOTT
>
> Look. See? This is where we are. You know that much.

MICHAEL grabs the globe.

MICHAEL
Use this.

ELLIOTT closes the book and points to the United States on the globe.

ELLIOTT
See, we're here. Where are you from?

E.T. looks at the globe. He points out the window.

GERTIE
I don't like his feet.

ELLIOTT
Shhh. They're only feet. He's trying to tell us something.

ELLIOTT opens the atlas again. It opens to a drawing of the solar system. E.T. stops ELLIOTT from turning the page. ELLIOTT points to the globe and to the planet Earth in the drawing. E.T. points to the drawing and then out the window.

ELLIOTT
Yeah. Earth. Home.

E.T. takes the clay and begins rolling balls. E.T. places five clay balls on the solar system drawing.

MICHAEL
He can't count.

ELLIOTT
Wait.

E.T. points to the map, then to the balls. He points to the globe and to ELLIOTT, and to one small ball and himself. ELLIOTT shivers, one of the "cosmic" shivers that run up your spine.

ELLIOTT
(softly) Oh, no.

MICHAEL
Elliott?

The balls lift off of the book. They rise in the air above the children's heads and they begin to spin, to orbit, really, five of them around the one larger "sun" ball. E.T. points to the balls, then points out the window. He looks at the children.

120   **CLOSE: THE CHILDREN**   120
Shock, horror, and realization on their faces.

WIDER: E.T. AND CHILDREN

E.T. points to the same small ball and back to himself.

> ELLIOTT
> Oh, no.

> MICHAEL
> Elliott?

> ELLIOTT
> Oh, no.

Suddenly, the balls fall to the floor. E.T. turns his head in the direction of the window. HARVEY's ears suddenly perk up and he looks to the window. ELLIOTT shivers. His face reflects E.T.'s fear.

> MICHAEL
> What is it?

> ELLIOTT
> I don't know. Something scary.

> GERTIE
> What?

> ELLIOTT
> I don't know!

E.T. is on his feet. He tries to push the children into the closet. They immediately oblige him, curious and confused. GERTIE is still holding the geranium.

122   INT. CLOSET — NIGHT   122

E.T. backs into the "living area" of the closet. ELLIOTT slips out of the closet.

123   INT. CLOSET — NIGHT   123X

ELLIOTT quietly sneaks down the stairs and out the front door.

124   EXT. BACK YARD — NIGHT   124

ELLIOTT runs up the flagstone stairs. The red gate light is on. Hear the sound of keys.

125   EXT. BACK YARD GATE — NIGHT   125X

ELLIOTT stands at the gate, illuminated by the red light. He can hear the sound of keys and the steady ticking of a geiger counter.

125 A   REVERSE   125A

Into the darkness... see nothing.

126   EXT. BACK YARD — NIGHT   126

ELLIOTT closes the gate. Deep fear is visible in his

face. The sound of keys grows louder. **ELLIOTT** looks up at the dark, starry sky.

127   **EXT/INT. ELLIOTT'S ROOM**   127

View of a night sky filled with stars.

The view pulls in to **ELLIOTT** 's room. **ELLIOTT** is sitting on his top bunk, silhouetted against his window, wrapped in a blanket. His focus is unchanging, directed at the closet.

His door opens, and **MICHAEL**, clad in pajamas, comes in and climbs up next to him. Together they stare in the direction of the closet. The camera moves across the filthy room and toward the closet. The door is open, and a dim light can be seen.

128   **INT. THE CLOSET — NIGHT**   128

The camera moves into the closet, past the barricades of storage boxes and stuffed animals. E.T. sits in his living area, looking through one of **GERTIE**'s **ABC** books. He turns the pages slowly, stopping at the letter 'B,' for **BOY**. E.T. touches the drawing of the small boy.

E.T. looks up, and his attention is drawn to the geranium now placed under the closet window. E.T. stares at the flower.

129   **REVERSE: THE FLOWER**   129

Before our eyes, the flower turns on its stem. As it faces E.T., it straightens. In a burst of life, its tight buds begin to open, suddenly blooming, bursting forth in brilliant red flowers.

130   **BACK: TO E.T.**   130

He strums his fingers on the drawing of the boy, and we hear him speak softly.

                         E.T.
               Elliott, Elliott.

FADE OUT

How to
Design a Movie Poster

What do lifelike dinosaurs, creatures from outer space, and a giant gorilla at the top of the Empire State Building have in common? They've all been the stars of movies—and their images have all been used on movie posters.

What is a movie poster? A movie poster is an eye-catching sign that announces a new film. It includes the title of the movie, a list of the stars, and an image from the movie. It is one of the ways a movie company advertises the film, and gets people interested in seeing it.

The tag line tries to convince the reader to go and see the movie.

The eye-catching image shows the star or a dramatic scene from the movie.

The title uses attention-grabbing letters that are easy to read.

ADVENTURE COMES TO LIFE

THE INDIAN IN THE CUPBOARD

A KENNEDY-MARSHALL PRODUCTION IN ASSOCIATION WITH SCHOLASTIC PRODUCTIONS PARAMOUNT PICTURES AND COLUMBIA PICTURES PRESENT ORIGINAL SCORE COMPOSED BY RANDY EDELMAN COSTUME DESIGNER DEBORAH L. SCOTT FILM EDITOR IAN CRAFFORD A FRANK OZ FILM THE INDIAN IN THE CUPBOARD HAL SCARDINO LITEFOOT LINDSAY CROUSE RICHARD JENKINS RISHI BHAT AND DAVID KEITH DIRECTOR OF PHOTOGRAPHY RUSSELL CARPENTER SPECIAL VISUAL EFFECTS AND ANIMATION BY INDUSTRIAL LIGHT & MAGIC SCREENPLAY BY MELISSA MATHISON EXECUTIVE PRODUCERS BERNIE WILLIAMS, ROBERT HARRIS AND MARTY KEITZ BASED UPON THE NOVEL BY LYNNE REID BANKS PRODUCED BY KATHLEEN KENNEDY, FRANK MARSHALL AND JANE STARTZ DIRECTED BY FRANK OZ

● The main actors, writer, director, and producer are listed in the credits.

1 Pick an Idea

When you think about movies, which ones pop into your head right away? Jot down four or five movie titles that come to mind. Think about what makes each movie memorable. Was the poster for each of the movies memorable, too?

If you were to make your own film, what kind of movie would it be? a mystery? a comedy? a science fiction adventure story? Think about a story line. Then write down your ideas for a catchy movie title. Decide which title will both fit your movie and grab an audience's attention. The title you choose will be an important feature of the movie poster you design.

TOOLS

- large piece of construction paper or posterboard

- art supplies

- newspapers and magazines

ACTION!

2 Write a Tag Line

A movie poster often has a tag line found above or below the title. It's a catchy sentence or phrase that tells more about the subject of the movie. Here is an example of a tag line:

SPACEFLIGHT 336
The intergalactic journey that changed the universe!

What can you tell about this movie from the title and tag line? Look at the movie section of a newspaper. Study the tag lines in the movie ads. Then write a few tag lines for your movie title. Decide which works best.

Tip Critics can play a part on movie posters, too. Include a quote from a review—a favorable one, of course!

3 Design Your Poster

Will the eye-catching image on your poster be of the main characters? a dramatic scene? several scenes? Think about what image will make people want to see your movie. Design your poster on scrap paper first. When you're satisfied, make your final design on posterboard or a large sheet of construction paper. Don't forget to include the title and the tag line.

SPACEFLIGHT 337

THE INTERGALACTIC JOURNEY THAT CHANGED THE UNIVERSE!

4 Give Credit

Who are the actors and actresses in your movie? You may want to give some friends in your class their first big movie role. List the stars of your movie on the poster. Did you write, direct, and produce this movie yourself? If so, give yourself credit!

Exhibit the posters you and your classmates created. Is there a type of movie that seems to be especially popular? Maybe some day, one of the ideas will appear on the big screen!

If You Are Using a Computer ...

Create your movie poster in the Poster format on the computer. Experiment with font sizes and styles for the title and credits.

THINK

What other kinds of advertising could you use to promote a movie?

Ellen Poon
Computer Artist ▶

Creative talent brings
fantastic stories to life.

Coming Attractions

Discover how special-effects experts make movie magic. Meet Ellen Poon, a computer artist who makes the impossible possible.

Read about the different talents needed to get comic books from the idea stage into your hands. Then learn what it takes to become an illustrator.

TM & © 1995 Marvel

PROJECT

Write a movie scene for a story of your very own.

The Long Lost Treasure of Volcano Island

Script by Pat Varga

From *Industrial Light & Magic*
The Art of Special Effects
by Thomas G. Smith

ENGINEERING OF

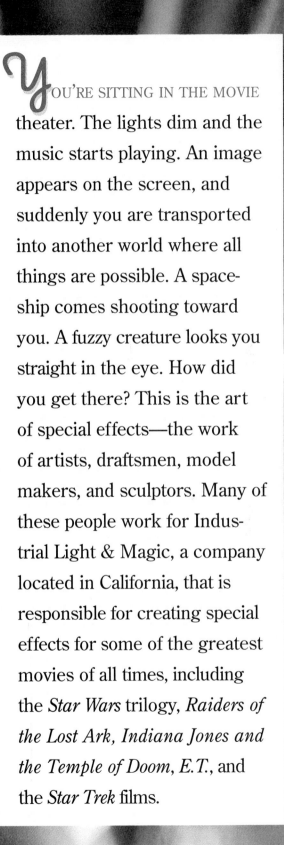

A MODEL

YOU'RE SITTING IN THE MOVIE theater. The lights dim and the music starts playing. An image appears on the screen, and suddenly you are transported into another world where all things are possible. A spaceship comes shooting toward you. A fuzzy creature looks you straight in the eye. How did you get there? This is the art of special effects—the work of artists, draftsmen, model makers, and sculptors. Many of these people work for Industrial Light & Magic, a company located in California, that is responsible for creating special effects for some of the greatest movies of all times, including the *Star Wars* trilogy, *Raiders of the Lost Ark, Indiana Jones and the Temple of Doom, E.T.*, and the *Star Trek* films.

A GROUP OF PEOPLE REVIEW THE MODELS, FROM RIGHT TO LEFT: MODEL SHOP SUPERVISOR LORNE PETERSON, ARCHIVIST DEBBIE FINE, GEORGE LUCAS, PRODUCER HOWARD KAZANJIAN, MODELMAKER CHARLIE BAILEY, AND ILM GENERAL MANAGER TOM SMITH (AUTHOR).

SPECIAL EFFECTS DEFINITIONS

The world of special effects is full of words not found in many other places. Use these words to help you while reading this selection.

articulation: the way in which parts are joined together

fortified: increased the strength and usefulness of

incandescent: glowing or white with heat

pylon: a support apparatus used for miniature models

vacu-form: process by which plastic is heated up and draped over an object, and the air completely removed, so that the hot plastic takes the shape of the original object

A MODEL made for an ILM film has to be more than just a good-looking piece of work. First, there are the practical considerations: on a big film an important model will be used every day for months, subjected to hot lights, sometimes rough handling, and occasionally collisions with computer-controlled cameras. For these reasons, the models cannot be too delicate or they will never survive the daily stress and will become a constant source of trouble during shooting. They are, therefore, much more durably constructed than models made for museums or crafted by the typical amateur hobbyist. The strength begins inside: the interior is

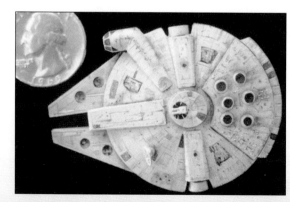

A TINY **MILLENNIUM FALCON,** NOT MUCH LARGER THAN A QUARTER.

92

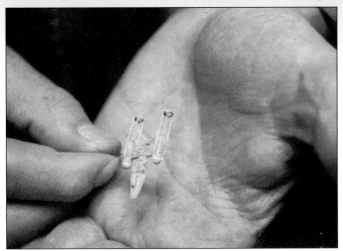

A TINY Y-WING MODEL.

(right)
MODELMAKER
PAUL HUSTON
SETS UP THE
MINIATURE CITY
SET FOR
EXPLORERS.

fortified with a metal frame that is engineered to maintain the integrity of the model's shape and provide support when attached to the mounting pylons. Exterior articulation for the outer skin of the model cannot be so delicate that it requires constant maintenance. Often the exterior begins as a collage of hundreds of small plastic fragments, which then serves as a master from which a mold is made; this is the basis for vacu-form rugged panels that are applied to the exterior of the final model.

During filming, a model must be supported on a specially built pylon. When shooting from the front, the support pylon is mounted on the rear; when we look at the model from the rear, the pylon is mounted on the front. When seen from above or below, the pylon is attached to the non-camera side of the model and held solidly during the filming. These multiple support locations require engineering considerations that the

home hobbyist does not have to deal with. Panels on the exterior skin of the spaceships snap off to reveal each mounting point, and there may be as many as four mounting spots on one model. The pylon upon which the model is mounted is also quite complex: the more sophisticated versions have special blue lighting that surrounds them so that they will blend with the blue screen that serves as a background and therefore become invisible after being optically composited into a final shot. The pylon also contains precision motors that interface with the camera's computer, allowing the spaceship to move on several preplanned axes while being photographed. Apparent model moves are accomplished by moving the camera back and forth on its long track. With the combined capability of the camera and the pylon movements, the operator is able to put the spaceship through an almost unlimited number of maneuvers.

(right) THE MODEL OF THE SPIDER, USED ON **EXPLORERS**, AS IT ARRIVES FOR FILMING AT THE ILM STAGE.

Most models are filled with electronics. There are the lights in the engine pods on spaceships, lights that shine from the "windows" of the craft, and the concealed miniature motors that control wing flaps, puppet pilot head turns, and any other mechanical action that might be required of a model. The modelmakers at ILM have had to be very innovative in the way lights are installed in these spaceships because there is very limited space in the average model to accommodate normal lighting. Though miniature incandescent bulbs are sometimes used, bundles of glass fiber optics (like a braid of hair) were used on the X-wing fighters, Y-wing fighters, and the TIE fighters. They were also used for the Star Destroyer, and Vader's Destroyer in *Star Wars* and *The Empire Strikes Back* because of the ship's limited space and the need for thousands of tiny window lights.

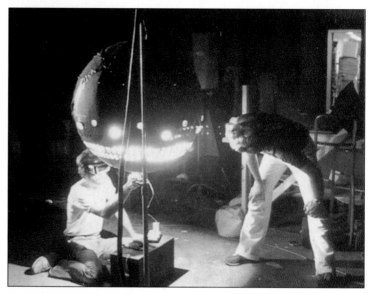

(above) DETAIL OF THE **E.T.** SHIP'S INTERIOR LIGHTING, USING QUARTZ HALOGEN SOURCES.

(above) VISUAL EFFECTS SUPERVISOR DENNIS MUREN AND TECHNICIAN MARTY BRENNEIS, WITH THE INNER SKELETON OF THE **E.T.** SHIP.

(left) CAMERAMAN PATRICK SWEENEY TAKES A METER READING FOR AN **EXPLORERS** MINIATURE SET.

Light emanates from one source at one end of the large bundle, and at the other end each small strand is then brightly illuminated. The bundle was taken apart with the small hairlike fibers distributed to the interior of the small portholes of the ship, so when the fibers were illuminated, thousands of small lights shone like the lights of Manhattan on a clear night. Their great number and small size helped to communicate the idea of a large ship.

MODELMAKER CHARLIE BAILEY EXAMINES A SMALL PROTOTYPE OF THE **E.T.** SHIP.

With all this mechanical and lighting gear crammed into these models, they have another unexpected need: air conditioning! Almost every model is cooled with a compressed air heat-extraction system. Without this system, most models would melt from the internal heat of the electronic gear combined with the heat from the intense stage lighting that is focused on the model during photography.

(above) MODELMAKER BILL GEORGE WORKS ON A SPACESHIP MODEL.

FROM LEFT: **EMPIRE STRIKES BACK** MODELMAKERS STEVE GAWLEY, DAVE CARSON, PAUL HUSTON; BACK ROW: LORNE PETERSON, MARC THORPE, MICHAEL FULMER; MIDDLE ROW: EASE OWYEUNG, WESLEY SEEDS, SAM ZOLLTHEIS; FOREGROUND: CHARLIE BAILEY.

MODELMAKER STEVE GAWLEY WORKS
ON A STAR DESTROYER.

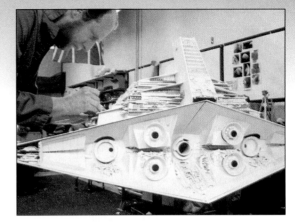

When the Death Star was built for *Return of the Jedi,* large illuminated areas were made of brass plates that were etched to create holes where windows were to appear, and then backed with neon light tubes. This system was also used on many of the variety of spaceships created for the ILM *Star Trek* projects. Again this technique created the appearance of many light sources, but it also turned out to be less time-consuming than the fiber optical system, since there were no small fibers to be connected to the portholes.

(left) MODELMAKER CHARLIE BAILEY WORKS ON THE INTERIOR OF THE **STAR DESTROYER.**

(left) THE ILM **E.T.** CREW, FROM LEFT TO RIGHT: MICHAEL McALISTER, DIRECTOR STEVEN SPIELBERG, PAT SWEENEY, KEN SMITH, MICHAEL FULMER, PRODUCER KATHLEEN KENNEDY, WARREN FRANKLIN AND DENNIS MUREN.

INTERIOR OF A MODEL FROM **STAR TREK III: THE SEARCH FOR SPOCK,** ILLUMINATED BY NEON LIGHTING.

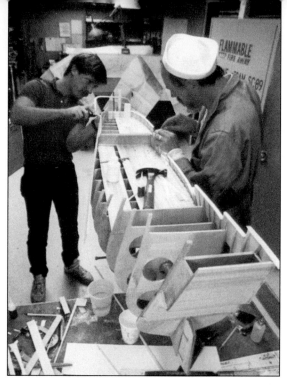

MODELMAKERS BILL GEORGE (LEFT) AND CHUCK WILEY (RIGHT) BUILD THE HULL FOR THE GALLEON SHIP IN **GOONIES.**

Though some models weigh only a few ounces and have no lights or mechanical parts, many models are complicated devices weighing hundreds of pounds and requiring a crew of stagehands to move them from place to place. When a model is delivered for shooting on the stage, it also comes with a substantial package of electronics to control the internal functions. These controls allow the model's miniature motors to interface with the computer that runs the camera. In addition, a power supply for the model's lighting is associated with each model.

Each model is a marvel of engineering and artistry. It is hoped by *Star Wars* fans the world over that someday these unique objects will be displayed in a museum for close inspection. When that day comes, viewers will be astounded that these models look even better in real life than they do on film.

MODELMAKER RANDY OTTENBERG WORKS ON THE RIGGING FOR THE GALLEON SHIP IN **GOONIES.**

(right) THE FINAL COMPOSITE SHOT SHOWING THE E.T. SPACESHIP HOVERING ABOVE THE TOWN.

Ellen Poon

Computer Artist

She makes *ideas* come to *life* on the big *screen*.

You're sitting in a darkened movie theater. On the screen, an actor transforms into a shining silver robot before your eyes. It looks so real you're on the edge of your seat. But it's not real, it's a special effect—and the person behind it just might be Ellen Poon. Ellen Poon is a computer artist for Industrial Light and Magic. Her job is to bring the director's ideas for special effects to life. She makes this happen by using her imagination and her computer.

PROFILE

Name: Ellen Poon

Occupation: computer artist

Education: degree in computer science; also studied art, design, and animation

Favorite fantasy movie: *The Seventh Voyage of Sinbad*

Favorite cartoon character: Bugs Bunny

First movie she worked on: *Hook*, animating Peter Pan's shadow

QUESTIONS
for Ellen Poon

Here's how **Ellen Poon** *uses her* **computer** *to* *bring* *characters* *to* **life.**

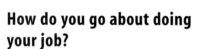

How do you do that?

After a lot of thinking! Sometimes I can spend weeks just coming up with an idea for an effect.

How do you come up with a good idea?

I put a lot of myself into the characters I create. Animation isn't animation unless it has spirit; it has to feel real. Sometimes I stand in front of the mirror and make funny faces. If you happen to walk past my office, you might think I'm kind of weird. But I'm really just acting out my characters.

How do you go about doing your job?

First, I read the script. Then I look at the storyboards, which are done by artists who work with the director of the movie. The storyboards are drawings that show what is supposed to happen in each frame. The director might have a special effect in mind for a scene. It's my job to create that effect.

Where else do you get your ideas?

Everywhere! I get ideas from watching cartoons, going to movies, and reading books. Sometimes ideas come to me quickly. I might suddenly wake up in the middle of the night and think, "Hey! That's what I'm going to do."

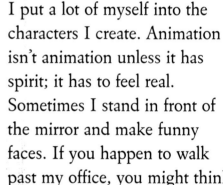

 After you decide what you want to create, how do you make it part of the movie?

 What qualities do animators need to have?

 A sense of humor is important. Sometimes you have to work until two in the morning. At times like that, it can be really hard to work unless you can laugh about it. A big part of what animators do is to make people laugh, so it's a good idea if you learn to laugh, too.

I turn to the computer. I have to make sure the effect matches the movements of the actor or actress. I work with the scene from the movie on my computer screen. I use my computer to "draw" the effect on top of the film and to make my drawings move. It can take weeks to get the effect just right.

Next, I work with a team to add light and color to the animated effect. If everything looks wonderful, we put all the effects together in a final process called compositing.

Tips **Ellen Poon's for Future Computer Artists**

 Computer technology is always changing. How do you keep up with it?

1 Keep on the lookout for news about computer animation.

2 Stay awake in math class! It's impossible to make objects on a computer move without understanding math.

 I do a lot of research. I read all the books that I can to keep up with changes in the field.

3 Study science. You can't animate a cartoon bird flying unless you know what makes real birds fly.

103

From **Funny Papers**

Behind the Scenes of the Comics

COMIC BOOKS
FOR FUN AND PROFIT

by Elaine Scott

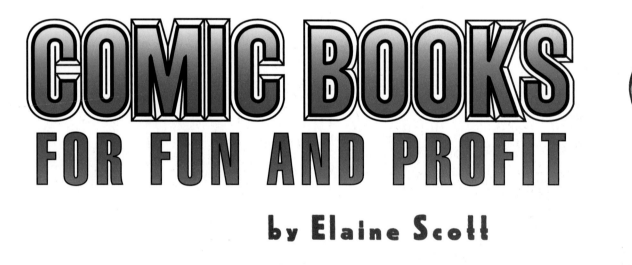

Chances are, your parents and grandparents had stacks of comic books when they were young. Perhaps you have a stack of your own right now.

Technically, the comic book began in 1911 when the popular *Mutt and Jeff* strips were gathered into book form and published. However, it was another twenty-two years before the comic book as we know it today really got started.

In 1933, two high school students, Jerry Siegel and Joe Shuster, became interested in a kind of writing called science fiction. They decided to put out their own magazine, which they produced by using their school's mimeograph machine. Jerry Siegel wrote stories about a superhero who could "hurdle skyscrapers...leap an eighth of a mile...raise tremendous weights...run faster than a streamlined train...and nothing less than a bursting shell could penetrate his skin!" Joe Shuster illustrated the character doing all of these things...and more. Siegel and Shuster called their stories "Reign of the Superman," and though the boys could not have known it at the time, they had created an American legend.

DC Comics was a relatively new comic book publishing company in 1938. In addition to publishing *Detective Comics*, DC decided to introduce another comic book in June of 1938. The new comic book was called *Action Comics*, and for $130, the publishers bought the rights to the Superman character from Jerry Siegel and Joe Shuster. The rest, as people say, is history. The Superman stories took the country by storm, and other comics with other superheroes soon followed.

Superman appeared as a comic book in 1938; by 1940, there were 60 new comic books on the newsstands of America. By 1941, there were 108 more, featuring the exploits of heroes with names such as Batman, Captain Marvel, Wonder Woman, Sub-Mariner, Flash Gordon, and Buck Rogers.

The world was a troubled place when *Superman* first appeared. Adolph Hitler's armies were on the march in Europe, and though the United States was not yet involved in the fighting, it was watching Nazi Germany with an anxious eye. Like the comic strips, the comic books began to reflect what was going on in American life. The United States officially entered World War II in December 1941, but by then, comic book heroes had been fighting the enemy for nearly two years. In fact, in February 1940, the Sub-Mariner was fighting Nazis on the cover of a Marvel comic book. The war progressed, and America's young men and women joined the armed forces. As patriotism filled the land, new comic books appeared with titles such as *Wings, Our Flag, The Eagle,* and *Captain America.* As their names indicate, all of these comics dealt with patriotic themes, as America struggled in World War II.

Of course, the main purpose of the comics has always been entertainment. War or not, people still wanted to laugh. In addition to the funny papers, new comic books appeared that helped readers do just that. Many of the characters in the new comic books were already famous from movie cartoons; others appeared for the first time in comic books, and only later became "stars" in movie theaters and on television. Mickey Mouse and Donald Duck were already popular when they appeared in comic book form.

Captain America's March 1941 debut

Spider-Man fights for literacy.

On the other hand, Archie Andrews and his friends Jughead, Veronica, Reggie, and Betty were created as comic book characters, and had their own animated television show much later.

Marvel Comics is the largest comic book publisher in the United States. It publishes more than one hundred comic books each month, but none is more popular than *The Amazing Spider-Man,* created by Stan Lee. Stan Lee began his comic book career as a teenager. In 1940, he joined Marvel Comics. During his long career, he has been head writer, art director, and editor-in-chief, and now he is the publisher. Despite the responsibilities that Mr. Lee has, he still writes the daily comic strip *The Amazing Spider-Man,* though others may write the adventures that appear in the comic books.

Spider-Man made his first appearance in August 1962 in a Marvel Comic called *Amazing Fantasy.* Poor Spidey, as he is affectionately called, almost didn't make it as a cartoon character, because some people at *Amazing Fantasy* thought that stories about a spider would be distasteful and because *Amazing Fantasy* was not a popular comic book. Stan Lee decided to put his new superhero on the cover, anyway. "Nobody cares what you put in a book that's going to die, so I threw in Spider-Man," Stan Lee has said. "I featured him on the cover and then forgot about him."

Stan Lee might have forgotten his new character, but the readers did not. Spider-Man did not die. Instead, sales of *Amazing Fantasy* jumped, and in less than a year *The Amazing Spider-Man* had his own comic book. Today *The Amazing Spider-Man* still appears in comic books, as well as in daily comic strips. He fights off villains and fights for literacy, as you see from the illustration from a special Spider-Man comic on this page.

When he appeared, Spidey was different from traditional comic book superheroes like Superman. Spider-Man had doubts, worries, even fears. The "humanizing" influence of Spider-Man eventually affected other superheroes. Even Superman changed from the Man of Steel to a hero who could cry, bleed, and even die! In late 1992, DC Comics announced that Superman would be killed at the hands of a character named Doomsday.

America's Favorite Web-Slinger

Since he first appeared on comic book pages in 1962, Spider-Man has become one of the most popular heroes of all time. Why? Spidey creators Stan Lee and Steve Ditko say it's because the character was one they had fun with. They enjoyed telling stories about the Spider-Man character, and their readers must have picked up on it.

"Spidey" is really Peter Parker, a teenager who was bitten by a radioactive spider. Now he has super powers that are enhanced when he wears his special costume.

Spider-Man

Beast

Iceman

Idea Man

Besides creating Spider-Man, comic book publisher Stan Lee collaborated with artists to create an amazing number of super heroes. Some of the characters Lee has given life to are the Incredible Hulk, Iron Man, the Fantastic Four, and the original X-Men, including Marvel Girl, Iceman, and Beast.

How does he get so many ideas? Lee says his biggest creative influences are the plays of William Shakespeare, different legends and myths, and authors like Mark Twain, Edgar Allan Poe, and Sir Arthur Conan Doyle, creator of Sherlock Holmes.

The Hulk

Fantastic Four

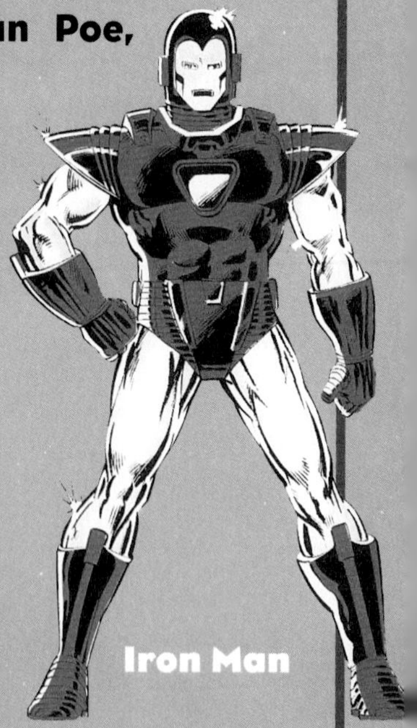

Iron Man

The text on the left document reads (partially legible):

> Even though we will probably use existing artwork, it would be nice if you co[uld]
> arranged so that the gatefold looked good as a mini-poster.
> On the front cover, we could use a picture of Stan Lee in the corner box.
> the corner box should be "3 QTR 1992." Since this issue is so heavily Spid[er]
> might want to consider using something other than the Spidey 30th anni[versary]
> illustration for the UPC bar code box.
>
> **Inside Page #1**
> In the first panel, Stan Lee finds Spidey on a Manhattan rooftop (St[anding by a]
> chimney or something, lost in thought, starring at the sunset). Stan
> paternal) says something like "What's on your mind, son?" Spidey
> "I've been thinking, Stan..."
>
> In the second panel, Spidey hops down and tells Stan somethin[g like]
> years since Marvel created me. And I've had some incredible
> fantastic people, and seen my personal life tossed and turned
> more times than I can remember."
>
> In the third panel, we see Spidey talking, an image of his pr[evious]
> Spidey continues with something like: "For instance, after
> parents were dead, I suddenly learn this summer that the[y were]
> imprisoned in East Germany!
>
> In the fourth panel, Parker asks something like, "I suppose, wh[at]
> shoulder... I've got what it takes to continue for another 30 year[s]
> "Without a doubt..."
>
> In the fifth panel, Stan explains to [Parker] "When
> you interesting super powers, but also a three-di[mensional]
> change and evolve -- from one story to the next,
> next. It soon became the magic formula for su[ccess]
>
> In the sixth panel, Spidey asks Stan: "How d[o]
> and pulls out a report and says, "Just take a l[ook]
> quarter!"
>
> **Inside Page #2**
> This page consists of typeset commenta[ry]
> in the form of a memo to all sharehold[ers]
> show that this page has been typeset c
> but without the Spider-Man drawing
> make sure we talk about the Spider-
> quarter and Spider-Man 2099 in th[e]

Comic books begin with a story outline and a rough pencil sketch.

The news caused much commotion and comment in America's newspapers and on television news shows. On October 4, 1992, the prestigious *New York Times* ran an editorial commenting on the Man of Steel's death. The writer ended the piece by noting, "Doubtlessly, DC Comics will see to it that Superman is subsequently born again; he's too big a part of the business to stay dead." Actually, in 1993, *four* Supermen returned, in four separate issues of the comic book, teasing readers with new questions about his identity.

Unlike comic strips, which rely on a syndicate to get them into readers' hands, the comic book is published by a company. At Marvel, as at all publishers, the story comes first. Creating the story is often a group effort by the editor, the writer, and the artist. Those three people meet together to discuss story ideas. Then the writer produces an outline of the story and sends it on to the artist, or penciler, as that person is called in the comic book business. The penciler draws a rough draft of each page of the comic book, based on the writer's outline.

This rough draft is called a storyboard. As in a comic strip, the action takes place in panels and the dialogue is in balloons—but the balloons are left empty at this point.

When everyone—the editor, the artist, and the writer—is satisfied with the storyboards for each page, the pages go back to the writer to decide on the exact words for the balloons. Next comes a rough pencil dummy to show the page layout; then a final pencil drawing of each page is made. A photostat, or photographic copy, is made of that pencil drawing, and the pages are then ready for the next step—inking. Ink artists carefully go over the pencil artist's work, using permanent black ink; then the pages go to a letterer, who inserts the dialogue in the balloons. Finally, the pages are ready to be colored, and there is a separate artist, called a colorer, to do that work. The art for the cover is painted, and the comic

Pencilers do a final drawing of the rough sketch.

The final pencil drawing goes to an inker.

After the picture is inked, the story is lettered in balloons.

The cover and interior pages are hand-colored by an artist.

is ready to go to a production facility to be printed.

Traditionally, comic books have been inexpensive reading material. The first ones cost ten cents each. Today's comics still cost far less than a paperback book. In order to keep the cost down, comic books are printed on inexpensive paper, and they have soft covers. Even though today's comic books are far better in quality than the first ones were, they are still easily ruined. Through the years, millions of copies of comic books have been thrown away—because they became tattered and torn, or because someone grew up and got tired of his collection.

Some people, however, saved their comic books, putting them in boxes and trunks and lugging them up to attics. Between 1937 and 1953, Edgar Church, who lived in Colorado, collected comic books. He stored them in eight-foot-high stacks in a dark room.

TM & © 1995 Marvel

The climate in Colorado is dry, which is perfect for preserving paper, and Edgar Church's comic book collection was perfectly preserved. Today each comic book in the Church collection looks as if it was just brought home from a newsstand.

Comic book collecting has always been a hobby, but now it is big business. There are conventions all across the country where people come to look at comic books, buy, sell, and trade them. A comic from the Edgar Church collection is the most expensive kind of comic a collector can own. In December 1991, Sotheby's, an internationally famous auction house, held an auction of comic books and comic art. An April 1937 ten-cent copy of *Detective Comics* that was in Edgar Church's collection sold for $16,500. The May 1939 issue of *Detective Comics* has on its cover: "Starting this issue: the amazing and unique adventures of THE BAT-MAN!" That comic was not part of the Edgar Church collection, but it was in very fine condition, and it sold for $55,000 at the same auction. In all, $1,205,905 in comic books and comic art was sold that day. Comic art may not hang on the walls of our most famous museums, but collectors are aware of its value. Today comic books are collected for fun *and* for profit.

A Spider-Man collector's treasure trove

Fan Mail

Marvel receives hundreds of letters from readers every week. Loyal fans send compliments, criticisms, and story ideas. Invariably, they catch minor errors that creep into the books—typographical errors, mistakes in the coloring of costumes, illogical plot details. Most often, though, fans write to tell the editors, writers, and artists how much they enjoy the comics.

When fourteen-year-old Billy Fraser, a devoted fan and collector, read in **Marvel Age** that the book **Five Fabulous Decades of the World's Greatest Comics** was in preparation, he offered to contribute an essay about why he loves comics. Billy owns more than five hundred comics, most of them Marvel books. "I went through a Hulk phase," he explains, "but now I'm most enthusiastic about Spider-Man, because he is so realistic and believable. For example, it's **really** interesting that he and Mary Jane are thinking about starting a family."

Like many fans his age, Billy would like to grow up to be a Marvel editor or writer—he is afraid that his drawing isn't good enough to qualify him to be an artist. But whatever happens, Billy's commitment to comics is firm. "I hope I never grow out of comics," he says. "My father grew up with Spidey and now I am, too. Spidey is really cool—that's what matters."

Why I Like Comics

I think that comics are great. Where else can you get action, excitement, fantasy and an intriguing plot all rolled into one?

Did you ever just stop and think what it would be like to be able to fly? It would be INCREDIBLE. Comics make it possible for me to see what it would be like to lift a truck, to have telepathy, to be indestructible. With comics, the possibilities are endless. That is what makes them so great: You can do anything in a comic.

And when comics get exciting, they get REAL exciting. I mean, blood-flowing, heart-racing, eye-popping excitement. Like, "Is he dead?" or "Will the hero win or lose?" or just plain, "How will the story end?"

I particularly like stories where super heroes meet and clash. One of my most serious investments was for <u>Amazing Spider-Man</u> #201, where The Punisher and Spidey have a temporary, but awful misunderstanding. It's a cool book.

And I also like the different characters in comics. They each have their own personalities, their own way of dealing with problems and their own lives. Some are stubborn, some are easy-going, some are loners and some are team-workers.

Plus I LOVE comic book art. Rippling muscles, dramatic poses, detailed facial expressions. All of it. A character's pose can make a scene look important, but it can also make that same scene look like an everyday get-together. Expressions and muscles can make a character look deranged, angered or pained. The colors in the artists's pictures can also set the mood; bright colors represent happiness, while darker ones represent gloominess.

All of these things are reasons I like comics. And as long as those are around, I'll be a collector.

Billy Fraser

Billy Fraser, age 14
Damariscotta, Maine

compiled and edited by
Pat Cummings

Talking
with
Artists

Conversations
with Victoria Chess · Pat Cummings · Leo and Diane Dillon · Richard Egielski · Lois Ehlert · Lisa Campbell Ernst · Tom Feelings · Steven Kellogg · Jerry Pinkney · Amy Schwartz · Lane Smith · Chris Van Allsburg and David Wiesner

compiled and edited by Pat Cummings

Interview

Tom Feelings

AWARD
WINNING

Book

My Story

Birthday: May 19, 1933

Although I've been drawing since I was four or five years old, my earliest memory of an interest in telling stories with pictures was around the age of nine. Until then, I had mainly copied characters from comic books or from newspaper funnies. I would invent plots, make up stories, and create my own characters for each new story.

I remember my mother helping me in all this by folding many sheets of blank paper in half and then stitching them together, at the fold, on her sewing machine. Then she would tell me to "draw her a book." I would fill up these "mama-made books" from the front cover to the back with my drawings.

116

I heard about an artist who was teaching at the Police Athletic League (P.A.L.) in my Brooklyn neighborhood and I went right over. There I met Mr. Thipadeaux, who was not only a real live working artist, he was a BLACK ARTIST—the first I had ever met.

I showed him all of my drawings. He immediately discouraged me from copying from comic books. He said, "Tom, drawing from your own imagination is good, but you can also bring something unique to your art by drawing and painting the world right around you—the people and places right in front of you, and the things you see every day. It is important that you see that, and try and show that, too."

With his encouragement I began to create posters for the P.A.L. sports events. I did watercolor sketches from my window, drawings from the P.A.L. window, and my first oil paintings—pictures of my mother and aunt.

Mr. Thipadeaux praised my new work. He always pushed me to do better and said he expected much more from me. Sometimes he irritated me by making me draw things over and over. He'd say, "Tom, you need discipline. Only hard work will develop your skills so that you can finally put down on paper not just what you see, but also what you *feel* about the subjects you draw and paint. One day you'll thank me for pushing you so hard." What I liked most about Mr. Thipadeaux was that he always treated me like an adult and constantly let me know that he had confidence in me.

Around this time, the art teacher in school gave us a special class assignment. She assigned a report for Negro History Week on two black historical figures. I would have to do research at the library. I was more than familiar with the library's children's room, having spent many days and hours reading Grimm's fairy tales and books like that, books that took me to a

never-never land, far from Brooklyn, on an imaginary journey . . . to places that only existed for me in the pages of those books. But this assignment dealt with real people, two black men out of my historical past: George Washington Carver, a scientist, and Booker T. Washington, an educator.

I had to look in a place I had never been—the library adult section. A librarian directed me to a small room where all the books about African-Americans were kept. I glided into this wonderful room, packed full of books on the Black Experience. Here for the first time I read about people who looked like me. I eagerly read through the material on the two prominent men and then discovered many more black people from a past I barely knew existed. Frederick Douglass, Harriet Tubman, Sojourner Truth, Hannibal . . . on and on.

When I saw paintings in the few books with art in them by black artists, questions arose in my mind. But no one was there to answer them. I looked at those pictures for hours, trying to imagine what each artist had felt . . . I thought I could somehow get answers by staring at the art. The short biographical statements about each artist told me very little about their lives. Had they come out of a community like mine? When did they start drawing and painting the life around them? Did they copy from magazines and books as I did—books that had no images of black people in them at all?

So many questions were left unanswered, until I found the poetry section and the poems of

Langston Hughes. His words seemed to light up all those corners of my mind. His word images connected me to that past I was reading about, to the present I was living, and even to the life it turned out that I would experience in the future. For, in his poetry, I could *see* the places and *feel* the faces I was familiar with as clearly as if he had painted them—just for me.

Above all, he showed so much love for his own people and his words spoke directly to that feeling. I yearned to express myself, just like him, with my art. I knew then that one day I wanted to illustrate those books that I had yet to see. I had a constant reminder of that desire every time I thought of Langston's poem "My People."

My People

The night is beautiful, so the faces of my
people. The stars are beautiful, so the eyes
of my people. Beautiful, also, is the sun.
Beautiful, also, are the souls of my people.

1. Where do you get your ideas from?

I get my ideas from the life around me, by constantly looking at, observing, and taking in all I can see and hear, especially through contact with people—directly and indirectly. I also get ideas by watching films and television and by reading articles and books that interest me. I bring all of this, I believe, to any story I'm going to illustrate.

I read the text of the story thoroughly, looking for visual clues. I jot them down and then select the ideas that best capture what is happening in that part of the story. From these ideas I develop sketches and layouts into final drawings.

2. What do you enjoy drawing the most?

Primarily people, and all those things related to and affected by human beings.

3. Do you ever put people you know in your pictures?

Yes. In one book I illustrated, *Song of the Empty Bottles*, the main character was a boy about eight years old. He was the same age as my nephew at that time. So I photographed my nephew in different positions and angles. I focused especially on his face and head. I used these photos as reference material so that I would be able to maintain the same likeness of character throughout the book.

I did the same kind of thing with another boy, whom I used as a model for the book *A Quiet Place*.

4. What do you use to make your pictures?

I use different materials. I start with pencil, and sometimes pen and ink, to do the layouts, in which I indicate what will happen on the page, where the figures will appear. Then I do the drawings and finished line art. I later paint into these drawings with colored inks, tempera paints, or colored pencils. And sometimes I prefer mixing all these media as I transform the drawings into completed illustrations.

5. How did you get to do your first book?

Many years ago, when I returned from a trip to Africa, I went to the book publishers with my portfolio, filled with samples of my published and unpublished artwork. I showed them this art so they could get a feeling for the kinds of work I did. The pieces I chose to put in my portfolio showed my particular style and especially the subject matter I most enjoyed doing.

Soon, one art director called me, saying he had a story that he felt was right for me. It was about an African boy who wanted to become a master drummer and play for the Oba (the king). The book was called *Bola and the Oba's Drummers*. I read it, liked it, and decided to illustrate it—that was it.

**Unpublished Piece: From the Personal Collection of Tom Feelings. 1991.
Colored pencils and collage papers, 17" X 9".**

How to
Write a Movie Scene

Create a scene for *your own* blockbuster movie.

Dinosaurs! Extra-terrestrials! Superheroes! Who are the characters in your favorite movie? What are some of your favorite scenes from the movies? When a writer works on a screenplay, he or she works on it scene by scene. For each scene, the writer has to decide what the action will be, what characters will be present, and what the dialogue will be. Each scene of a movie is like a chapter in a book. It is an important part of a larger piece, and its purpose is to move the action and plot along.

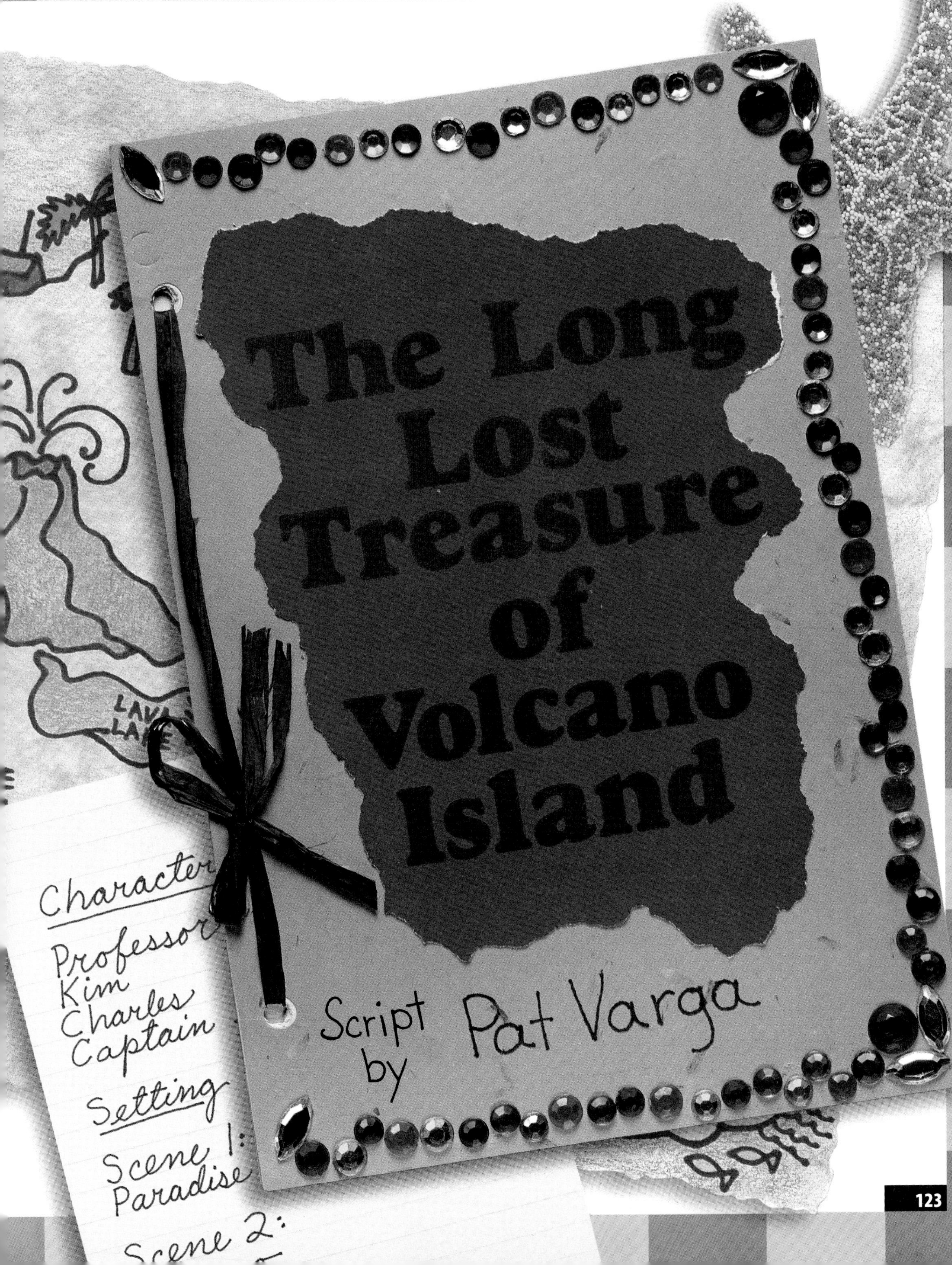

The Long Lost Treasure of Volcano Island

Script by Pat Varga

Character

Professor
Kim
Charles
Captain

Setting

Scene 1:
Paradise

Scene 2:

The first thing you need is a great idea for a movie. Will it be a science fiction movie? a sports story? a comedy? Your movie could also be based on a book you've recently read. After you've come up with an idea, write a paragraph or two telling about your movie. Who are the characters? What is the plot? Where does the story take place? Write enough so that you have a summary of the movie.

TOOLS

- paper and pencil

- art supplies

Next, think about which scene from your movie you'd like to write. It might be the scene in which your characters first meet. Or it could show them escaping from trouble, or winning a contest, or making up after an argument.

Then think about where in the movie your scene will take place. It may be the first scene, the exciting climax, or the last scene.

Finally, think about the characters who will appear in the scene. Make a list of them and write a short character description next to each name.

Before you begin to write, you might want to ask yourself:

- Do I know what will happen in my scene and who will be in it?

- Does my scene have a beginning, middle, and an end?

- Does my scene try to tell about too many events?

2 | Set Up the Scene

Now it's time to write your scene. First, write a brief introduction that lists the characters and tells the setting.

Next comes the dialogue. Begin with the character's name and what he or she says. As you're writing, try to imagine how your character is feeling. Is he or she angry, sad, happy, frightened? If you're having trouble making the dialogue sound natural, it might help to say the lines aloud.

Include stage directions for the character. You have to let the actor know when the character should run across the street or act as if he or she just heard a loud noise. As with the introduction, make sure the stage directions are set off from the dialogue.

Tip To make sure that the introduction and directions don't get confused with the dialogue, you can put them in parentheses, underline them, or highlight them in some other way.

How Am I Doing?

Before you go any further, look over your work and ask yourself these questions:

- Did I come up with a movie idea that will interest others?

- Did I create real-life dialogue for the scene?

- Did I write easy-to-understand stage directions?

Revise the Scene

Screenwriters often revise their work in its early stages. Sometimes screenwriters ask actors to read a scene aloud, and they discuss it afterward.

Hold a reading of your own. Ask classmates to read the different parts. Then discuss ways to improve your scene.

Some questions you may want to ask both yourself and the actors include:

- Does the scene make sense? Was any important information left out?

- Did the dialogue sound real? How could it be improved?

- Was the scene too long or too short? What could be added or left out?

After the discussion, rework your scene.

4 Put It Together

Here are some suggestions you can use to put your movie scene into final form.

- Create a title page. If you want, you can illustrate your title page.

- Include a cast of characters. Write a brief description of each character.

- Describe the setting and mood of the scene. Remember to include the time of day.

You may also want to put on a performance of your scene for your class. Choose classmates to play the parts. You can be the director. Make or bring from home any "props" you might need for your scene. Before you perform the scene, you may want to tell the audience a little about the movie and why the scene is important.

If You Are Using a Computer ...

Use your computer to make your revisions. If you decide to make major revisions in your scene, you might want to save each version.

CONGRATULATIONS

You have used your imagination to create all kinds of stories. Keep finding ways to put your creative talents to work.

Ellen Poon
Computer Artist ▶

Glossary

bal·loons
(bə lo͞onz′) *noun*
The usually round outlines that hold the words or thoughts of cartoon characters. ▲ **balloon**

be·spat·tered
(bē spat′ ərd) *adjective*
Splashed with a liquid. The cook's apron was *bespattered* with gravy.

bespattered

blotch·y
(bloch′ ī) *adjective*
Covered with large, oddly-shaped spots of color. My shirt was *blotchy* after I spilled paint on it.

col·lab·o·rat·ed
(kə lab′ ə rā′ təd) *verb*
Worked together with one or more other people. Tim and Maria *collaborated* on the book report.
▲ **collaborate**

col·lage (kə läzh′) *noun*
Artwork made of different materials glued on a surface.

> ### Word History
> **Collage** comes from the French word *coller*, which means "to glue."

com·pos·it·ed
(kəm poz′ i təd) *verb*
Combined with other parts to make something new.
▲ **composite**

cos·mic
(koz′ mik) *adjective*
Having to do with the universe beyond Earth.

crave (krāv) *verb*
To want something greatly. I *crave* lemonade on hot summer days.

daubs (dôbz) *noun*
Roughly-made pictures. Mom hangs my baby sister's *daubs* on the refrigerator. ▲ **daub**

dis·pute
(di spyo͞ot′) *noun*
A disagreement. We had a *dispute* over whose turn it was at bat.

dum·my (dum′ē) *noun*
A rough version of a page in a book, magazine, or newspaper. The dummy shows what the page will look like when it is finished.

en·gi·neered
(en jə nērd′) *verb*
Planned out.

ex·tra-ter·res·tri·al
(ek´ strə tə res´ trē əl)
noun
A being that comes from someplace other than Earth.

Fact File

The name E.T. is a shortened form of extra-terrestrial.

fangs (fangz) *noun*
Long, sharp teeth.
▲ **fang**

fangs

fi·ber op·tics
(fī´ bər op´tiks) *noun*
See-through threads of glass or plastic that conduct light.

fiber optics

gi·gan·tic
(jī gan´ tik) *adjective*
Of great size and power.

Thesaurus

gigantic

enormous
giant
huge

glow·er (glou´ ər) *noun*
An angry stare.

god·dess·es
(god´ is iz) *noun*
Female gods.
▲ **goddess**

grumped (grumpd)
verb
Complained.
▲ **grump**

Word Study

The word **grump** can take other forms in addition to the verb form. A *grump* (noun) is a person who constantly grumbles and complains. And someone who is *grumpy* (adjective) is in a bad mood.

a	add	o͝o	took	ə =
ā	ace	o͞o	pool	a in *above*
â	care	u	up	e in *sicken*
ä	palm	û	burn	i in *possible*
e	end	yo͞o	fuse	o in *melon*
ē	equal	oi	oil	u in *circus*
i	it	ou	pout	
ī	ice	ng	ring	
o	odd	th	thin	
ō	open	th	this	
ô	order	zh	vision	

Glossary

hue (hyoō) *noun*
A shade of color. He had shirts in every *hue* of green.

hue

il·lu·mi·nat·ed
(i loō' mə nā' təd) *adjective*
Brightly lit.

ink·ing (ing' king) *verb*
The act of drawing something in ink. ▲ **ink**

in·ter·face
(in' tər fās) *verb*
To communicate or share information.

jade green
(jād grēn) *adjective*
A blue-green color.

jux·ta·pos·es
(juk' stə pōz' iz) *verb*
Places side by side.
▲ **juxtapose**

lay·outs (lā' outs) *noun*
Plans or designs. In books, magazines, and newspapers, layouts show where the elements of the page (like photos, headlines, and type) will be placed when the page is finished.
▲ **layout**

mu·tant
(myoōt' nt) *noun*
A being that is physically different than normal because of changes in its basic structure.

mut·ter (mut' ər) *verb*
To complain angrily in a low voice.

myth·ic
(mith' ik) *adjective*
Based on fictional stories or legends that explain how things came to be.

nymphs (nimfs) *noun*
From mythology, female gods associated with nature. Nymphs were thought to live in mountains, forests, waters, and caves. ▲ **nymph**

op·ti·cal·ly
(op' ti kə lī) *adverb*
Using light-sensitive devices to get information for a computer.

pa·nels (pan' lz) *noun*
The sections of a comic book page. Panels separate the scenes in the story.
▲ **panel**

pig•ments
(pig′ ments) *noun*
Powdered substances that give color to paints and inks. ▲ **pigment**

Word History

Pigment is derived from the Latin word *pingere*, which means "to paint."

rant (rant) *verb*
To talk in a noisy, excited manner.

rave (rāv) *verb*
To talk wildly and without reason.

sa•cred
(sā′ krid) *adjective*
Deserving of honor and respect.

sto•ry•board
(stôr′ ē bôrd′) *noun*
A rough draft of a comic book that shows how the scenes will be set up.

syn•di•cate
(sin′ di kit) *noun*
A company that sells materials like comic strips to newspapers.

tentacles on an octopus

Fact File

The largest **syndicate** in the United States is United Media, which sells the comic strips "Peanuts" and "Garfield" to newspapers all over the world.

ten•ta•cles
(ten′ tə kəlz) *noun*
Long body parts used for touching or grasping that jut out from an animal's body and are usually located near the head or mouth. ▲ **tentacle**

ver•mil•ion
(vər mil′ yən) *noun*
A bright red-orange color.

vi•sion (vizh′ ən) *noun*
Something perceived in a dream.

yearned (yûrnd) *verb*
Longed for. Mark *yearned* to ride the prize horse. ▲ **yearn**

zapped (zapt) *verb*
Destroyed. ▲ **zap**

a	add	o͝o	took	ə =
ā	ace	o͞o	pool	a in *above*
â	care	u	up	e in *sicken*
ä	palm	û	burn	i in *possible*
e	end	yo͞o	fuse	o in *melon*
ē	equal	oi	oil	u in *circus*
i	it	ou	pout	
ī	ice	ng	ring	
o	odd	th	thin	
ō	open	t͟h	this	
ô	order	zh	vision	

Authors & Illustrators

Lloyd Alexander *pages 42–53*

This Philadelphia born author was an avid reader as a child. Some of his favorite books were tales of Greek mythology and the legends of the country of Wales. When he began writing in the 1950s, he decided to create his own myths and legends. His fantasy novels are widely read around the world, especially the series of books called the Prydain Chronicles, which includes the Newbery Award-winning novel *The High King*.

Shonto Begay *pages 18–21*

This poet, author, and artist is one of 16 children born to a Navajo medicine man in Arizona. He remembers growing up listening to his grandmother tell stories around the fire. Begay believes the traditional stories of his heritage have messages in them. After studying fine arts, he began to combine his paintings and stories in picture books in the hopes of sharing those messages with others.

"Stories are one way to preserve a good portion of your culture."

Mary Pope Osborne *pages 10–17*

The daughter of a U.S. Army colonel, this author spent most of her childhood moving from place to place. After graduating from college, she continued to travel. It was while she was on the road with her husband Will, an actor, that she started writing. Osborne says she feels like she takes an incredible journey each time she writes a book. She enjoys retelling the amazing stories of the ancient Greeks.

Steven Spielberg *pages 70–83*

This Academy Award-winning film director and producer has taken millions of movie goers to other worlds over the years. Working with Melissa Mathison's script, Spielberg used his talents to bring the story of E.T. to the screen, making it one of the most popular films of all time. Steven Spielberg's combination of amazing special effects and great stories has inspired the imagination of generations of viewers.

Lawrence Watt-Evans *pages 58–69*

Lawrence Watt-Evans has loved science fiction for as long as he can remember. By second grade, he was reading books by famous science fiction author Ray Bradbury. Now Lawrence Watt-Evans works full-time writing the kinds of stories he loves. He has won numerous science fiction awards. He lives in Maryland, where he writes novels and short stories, and collects comic books.

Books &

Author Study

More by Lloyd Alexander

The High King
In this Newbery Award-winning book, Taran the pig keeper and his friends must find a way to stop the evil and powerful Arawn from taking over the land.

The Philadelphia Adventure
This adventure is set during the 1876 Centennial Exposition. Vesper Holly foils a plot by the scheming Dr. Helvitius.

Time Cat
Jason and his pet cat travel through time in this series of stories that draw upon myths and folklore about cats from many different lands.

Fiction

Dinotopia
by James Gurney
A father and son are shipwrecked on an island. They soon discover that it is a fantastic place where dinosaurs and people live together in harmony.

Forest
by Janet Taylor Lisle
A girl finds a new world when she climbs high into the treetops.

The Hobbit
by J.R.R. Tolkein
In this classic fantasy, Bilbo Baggins (a hobbit) is persuaded by a wizard named Gandalf to try to capture a treasure that belongs to a dragon.

The Magical Adventures of Pretty Pearl
by Virginia Hamilton
Pretty Pearl and many other characters in this fast-paced and funny fantasy novel are based upon gods and heroes from African and African-American folklore.

Nonfiction

Almost the Real Thing
by Gloria Skurzinski
Technology can be used to create amazingly realistic experiences. This book reveals how virtual reality is used today and may be used in the future.

Film: How Are Movies Made?
by Richard Platt
Photos, diagrams, and facts about every step in the process of making a film come alive in this book.

Radical Robots: Can You Be Replaced?
by George Harrar
This timely reference book is packed with photos and facts about robots.

xMedia

 Videos

E.T., the Extra-Terrestrial
MCA Home Video
This Steven Spielberg film became an instant classic. See for yourself how realistic special effects combine with a strong plot and well-drawn characters to create a memorable, suspenseful story. (1 hr. 55 minutes)

From "Star Wars" to "Jedi"
Fox
This behind-the-scenes documentary reveals many of the secrets behind the special effects used in this series. (65 minutes)

The Incredible Shrinking Woman
Universal
In this funny science-fiction picture, Lily Tomlin stars as a woman who keeps getting smaller and smaller and smaller. (1 hr. 22 minutes)

Software

Destination: MARS!
Compt-Teach
(IBM-PC, Macintosh Plus)
Welcome to the year 2010! You are a recruit of the National Space Agency. How well you do will determine if you get to be the first human to land on Mars.

SimCity
Maxis
(Macintosh, IBM, Amiga)
Use maps of real and imaginary cities to create and run your own city.

Space Adventure
Knowledge Adventure
(IBM, Macintosh)
Beautiful graphics, amazing sound effects, and clear text help you create your own space adventures and learn more about conditions in outer space.

Magazines

Classical Calliope
Cobblestone Publishing
This magazine brings the ancient world to life with articles and stories about mythology and ancient history.

Odyssey
Cobblestone Publishing
Learn more about Earth and the other planets in this well-written and beautifully illustrated science magazine.

A Place to Write

Smithsonian Institution
National Museum of American History
Visitors Information Center
Constitution Avenue and 14th
Washington, D.C. 20560

Write for a brochure describing the exhibit "Information Age: People, Information and Technology."

Acknowledgments

Grateful acknowledgment is made to the following sources for permission to reprint from previously published material. The publisher has made diligent efforts to trace the ownership of all copyrighted material in this volume and believes that all necessary permissions have been secured. If any errors or omissions have inadvertently been made, proper corrections will gladly be made in future editions.

Cover: Mark Summers.

Interior: "The Golden Apples," "The Weaving Contest," and cover from FAVORITE GREEK MYTHS by Mary Pope Osborne, illustrated by Troy Howell. Text copyright © 1989 by Mary Pope Osborne. Illustrations copyright © 1989 by Troy Howell. Reprinted by permission of Scholastic Inc.

"Storm Pattern," "Grandmother," and cover from NAVAJO: VISIONS AND VOICES ACROSS THE MESA by Shonto Begay. Copyright © 1995 by Shonto Begay. Reprinted by permission of Scholastic Inc.

"The Fox and the Grapes," "The Grasshopper and the Ants" and cover from AESOP'S FABLES as retold in verse by Tom Paxton, illustrated by Robert Rayevsky. Text copyright © 1988 by Tom Paxton. Illustrations copyright © 1988 by Robert Rayevsky. Reprinted by permission of Morrow Junior Books, a division of William Morrow & Company, Inc.

"All Stories Are Anansi's" and cover from THE HAT-SHAKING DANCE AND OTHER ASHANTI TALES FROM GHANA by Harold Courlander, cover illustration by Enrico Arno. Copyright © 1957, 1985 by Harold Courlander. Reprinted by permission of the author.

"The Camel Dances," camel illustration, and cover from FABLES by Arnold Lobel. Copyright © 1980 by Arnold Lobel. Reprinted by permission of HarperCollins Publishers.

"The Tale of the Tiger's Paintbrush" and cover from THE REMARKABLE JOURNEY OF PRINCE JEN by Lloyd Alexander, cover illustration by Paul O. Zelinsky. Text copyright © 1991 by Lloyd Alexander. Illustration copyright © 1991 by Paul O. Zelinsky. Reprinted by permission of Dutton Children's Books, a division of Penguin Books USA Inc.

RENÉ MAGRITTE and caption THE SON OF MAN from Art & Man, April/May 1980. Copyright © 1980 by Scholastic Inc. THE CASTLE OF THE PYRENEES caption from Scholastic Art February 1992. Copyright © 1992 by Scholastic Inc. TIME TRANSFIXED caption and Scholastic Art® logo from Scholastic Art September/October 1993. Copyright © 1993 by Scholastic Inc. Reprinted by permission.

"How I Maybe Saved the World Last Tuesday Before Breakfast" by Lawrence Watt-Evans. Copyright © 1994 by Lawrence Watt-Evans. Reprinted by permission of the author. Cover illustration from BRUCE COVILLE'S BOOK OF ALIENS by Steve Fastner. Illustration copyright © 1994 by General Licensing Company, Inc. Used by permission of General Licensing Company, Inc.

Selection from ET film script. Copyright © by Universal City Studios, Inc. Courtesy of MCA Publishing Rights, a Division of MCA Inc. All rights reserved.

Poster from the film THE INDIAN IN THE CUPBOARD courtesy of Paramount Pictures.

Selection from INDUSTRIAL LIGHT AND MAGIC: THE ART OF SPECIAL EFFECTS by Thomas G. Smith. Copyright © 1986 by Lucasfilm, Ltd. (LFL). Reprinted by permission of Ballantine Books, a division of Random House, Inc.

"Comic Books for Fun and Profit" and cover from FUNNY PAPERS: BEHIND THE SCENES OF THE COMICS by Elaine Scott, photographs by Margaret Miller. Text copyright © 1993 by Elaine Scott. Photographs copyright © 1993 by Margaret Miller. Reprinted by permission of Morrow Junior Books, a division of William Morrow & Company, Inc.

"Marvel Fan Mail Letter" from MARVEL'S FIVE FABULOUS DECADES OF THE WORLD'S GREATEST COMICS by Les Daniels. Published by Harry N. Abrams, Inc. Copyright © 1991 by Marvel Entertainment Group, Inc. Reprinted by permission of Marvel Entertainment Group, Inc. All rights reserved.

"Tom Feelings" and cover from TALKING WITH ARTISTS compiled and edited by Pat Cummings. Jacket illustration copyright © 1992 by Pat Cummings. Reprinted with the permission of Simon & Schuster Books for Young Readers, an imprint of Simon and Schuster Children's Publishing Division. Text and photos copyright © 1992 by Tom Feelings. Reprinted by permission of the artist.

Cover from FAVORITE GREEK MYTHS retold by Mary Pope Osborne, illustrated by Troy Howell. Illustration copyright © 1989 by Troy Howell. Published by Scholastic Inc.

Cover from THE LOST STAR by H.M. Hoover. Cover illustration by Charles Mikolaycak. Copyright © 1979 by Viking Penguin, Inc. Published by Viking Penguin, a division of Penguin Books USA Inc.

Cover from THE PHANTOM TOLLBOOTH by Norton Juster, illustrated by Jules Feiffer. Illustration copyright © 1989, 1961 by Jules Feiffer. Published by Random House, Inc.

Cover from TUCK EVERLASTING by Natalie Babbitt. Illustration copyright © 1975 by Natalie Babbitt. Published by Farrar, Straus and Giroux.

Photography and Illustration Credits

Selection openers: Greg Couch.

Photos: All Tools in Workshops and Project © John Lei for Scholastic Inc. unless otherwise noted. pp. 2-3: © John Jensen for Scholastic Inc. p. 2 bl: © David Lawrence for Scholastic Inc.; ml: © John Lei for Scholastic Inc.; tl(inset): © 1996 Lucasfilm Ltd.; © John Lei for Scholastic Inc. p. 3 bc: © John Jensen for Scholastic Inc.; tc: © Lester Lefkowitz/Tony Stone Worldwide. p. 4 c: © Francis Clark Westfield for Scholastic Inc.; tc: © Lester Lefkowitz/Tony Stone Worldwide. p. 5 c: © Francis Clark Westfield for Scholastic Inc.; tc: © Lester Lefkowitz/Tony Stone Worldwide. p. 6 c: © Francis Clark Westfield for Scholastic Inc.; tc: © Lester Lefkowitz/Tony Stone Worldwide; tl: © 1996 Lucas Film Ltd. pp. 18-19 c: Courtesy America Hurrah, NYC. pp. 20-21 c: © Jerry Jacka. p. 21 tc: © THE SLEEPING GYPSY by Henri Rousseau, Museum of Modern Art, gift of Mrs. Simon Guggenheim. pp. 36-37 background: © Donald Higgs/Index Stock Photography Inc.; c: © John Curry for Scholastic Inc. p. 38 bl: © Stanley Bach for Scholastic Inc. p. 39 br: © John Jensen for Scholastic Inc. p. 54 c: © THE SON OF MAN by René Magritte/Giraudon/Art Resource, NY. p. 56 c: © THE CASTLE IN THE PYRENEES by René Magritte/Art Resource. p. 57 c: © TIME TRANSFIXED by René Magritte/The Art Institute of Chicago. p. 70 c: © 1988 Universal City Studios/Photofest. p. 71 bl: © Yoram Kahana/Shooting Star; ml: © Universal City Studios/Shooting Star; br: © Universal City Studios; mr: © Elisa Leonelli/Shooting Star; tc: © Universal City Studios/Photofest; tl: © Yoram Kahana/Shooting Star; tr: © 1986 Universal City Studios. p. 72 bl: © Universal City Studios/Photofest. p. 73 mr: © Universal City Studios/Photofest. p. 74 ml: © Universal City Studios/Everett Collection. p. 76 ml: © Universal City Studios/Photofest. p. 77 mr: © Universal City Studios/Everett Collection. p. 80 ml: © Universal City Studios/Everett Collection. p. 82 ml: © Universal City Studios/Everett Collection. p. 83 br: © Universal City Studios/Photofest. pp. 84-85: © John Curry for Scholastic Inc. p. 86 bc: © Stanley Bach for Scholastic Inc. p. 87 br: © John Jensen for Scholastic Inc. pp. 90-91 c: © 1996 Lucasfilm Ltd. p. 92 tl: © 1996 Lucasfilm Ltd.; br: © 1996 Lucasfilm Ltd. p. 93 tl: © 1996 Lucasfilm Ltd.; tr: EXPLORERS and STAR TREK III: © Paramount Pictures, used with permission. p. 94 tr: EXPLORERS and STAR TREK III: © Paramount Pictures, used with permission; mr: Copyright © by Universal City Studios, Inc. Courtesy of MCA Publishing Rights, a Division of MCA Inc. All rights reserved; br: Copyright © by Universal City Studios, Inc. Courtesy of MCA Publishing Rights, a Division of MCA Inc. All rights reserved; bl: EXPLORERS and STAR TREK III: © Paramount Pictures, used with permission. p. 95 tl: Copyright © by Universal City Studios, Inc. Courtesy of MCA Publishing Rights, a Division of MCA Inc. All rights reserved; tr: Copyright © by Universal City Studios, Inc. Courtesy of MCA Publishing Rights, a Division of MCA Inc. All rights reserved; br: Copyright © by Universal City Studios, Inc. Courtesy of MCA Publishing Rights, a Division of MCA Inc. All rights reserved; bl: Copyright © by Universal City Studios, Inc. Courtesy of MCA Publishing Rights, a Division of MCA Inc. All rights reserved. p. 96 tr: Copyright © by Universal City Studios, Inc. Courtesy of MCA Publishing Rights, a Division of MCA Inc. All rights reserved; mr: © 1996 Lucasfilm Ltd.; bl: © 1996 Lucasfilm Ltd. p. 97 tr: © 1996 Lucasfilm Ltd.; mr: © 1996 Lucasfilm Ltd.; bl: Copyright © by Universal City Studios, Inc. Courtesy of MCA Publishing Rights, a Division of MCA Inc. All rights reserved. p. 98 tl: EXPLORERS and STAR TREK III: © Paramount Pictures, used with permission; tr: Copyright © 1996 Warner Bros. Inc.